➤ *Time to Fly Free*

D0851114

"Judith Smith has approached a painful topic with sensitivity, hope, and inspiration. Her personal knowing means a path to freedom for the millions of abused women."

— Marilyn Mason
Author, *Facing Shame, Making Our Lives Our Own*, and *Seven Mountains*

"In this powerfully uplifting book, Judith Smith serves as a wise companion and guide to the courageous survivors on a journey to a life of hope and possibility. Her careful words offer a road map to anyone who dared to leave an abusive relationship and dares to continue on a path to a joyful, honest life."

— Michele Weldon
Domestic violence victim advocate and author, *I Closed My Eyes*

Lecturer, Northwestern University Medill School of Journalism

➤ Time to Fly Free

*Meditations for Those Who Have
Left an Abusive Relationship*

JUDITH R. SMITH

▨ HAZELDEN®

INFORMATION & EDUCATIONAL SERVICES

Hazelden
Center City, Minnesota 55012-0176

1-800-328-0094
1-651-213-4590 (Fax)
www.hazelden.org

Library of Congress Cataloging-in-Publication Data

Smith, Judith R.
   Time to fly free : meditations for those who have left an
   abusive relationship / Judith R. Smith.
      p. cm.
   Includes index.
   ISBN 1-56838-580-3
      1. Abused women—Psychology—Miscellanea.
2. Abused women—Rehabilitation—Miscellanea.
3. Victims of family violence—Psychology—Miscellanea.
4. Victims of family violence—Rehabilitation—Miscellanea.
5. Affirmations. I. Title.

HV1444 .S55 2001
158.1'28—dc21   00-054680

05 04 03 02 01   6 5 4 3 2 1

Cover art by David Spohn
Interior design by Wendy Holdman
Typesetting by Spaulding & Kinne

➤ Dedication

After having left an abusive relationship at some point in your life, you are continuing to show tremendous courage by your willingness and desire to stay free. You are living proof that impossibility exists only in the minds of those who don't know they can. Your success in stepping beyond what you thought you could do is an example to others who remain trapped in their despair. There was a way your life could be different, there was a way your life could be better. And you, in all your glory, are taking the steps to make that happen.

This book is dedicated to all of us who have survived and, most of all, to those who didn't.

—*Judith R. Smith*

➤ Acknowledgments

It is with my deepest and most sincere love, respect, and appreciation that I say thank you to the following people:

Fritz, the loving man who showed me it was possible to trust again and who taught me to enjoy and cherish the unlimited happiness of a loving, safe, and healthy relationship.

My family, who always believed in me and encouraged me to pursue my dreams.

Donna Z., Cynthia Jannsen, Russell Freidman, Gavin de Becker, Melody Beattie, and Gurumayi, intuitive people whose wisdom gave me insight and inspiration while writing this book.

My children, Lacey and Max, whose love and patience allowed me the time to write and who showed me that by protecting them, my most important job on this earth was being their mother.

God, my Spiritual Power, for taking me under the wing of grace, patience, and unconditional love until I found the strength and courage to spread my own wings and fly free into a life that surpassed my wildest dreams.

Acknowledgments

➤ Introduction

You have accomplished something magnificent! You've already had the courage to break free from an abusive relationship, and now you are ready to move on to the next phase, flying free. In this book, I will suggest specific activities that can increase your awareness and your perception—survival skills that probably have been damaged by the abuse you've endured. In abusive relationships, the person who suffered the abuse usually experiences a decrease or lack of growth in the areas of focus, concentration, awareness of danger, normal range of fear, and perception of reality. With the exercises in this book, you can begin to develop these skills in order to better understand your new life and to function more effectively in it. I'm not, by any means, saying that you must complete every activity if you are to stay free. If you follow my suggestions, however, the likelihood of this happening is increased significantly. Don't worry if you miss a day; do not skip ahead to catch up. Simply pick up the book and start where you left off.

If you find yourself having difficulty with any of my suggestions, or if they begin to trigger intense feelings that seem overwhelming, remember that this book is not intended to be used as your only source of support or education upon leaving your abuser. I strongly recommend that you seek professional assistance from a therapist, a counselor, or a support group. I might also add that it's of the utmost importance when choosing professional help that you find someone or someplace that specializes in domestic violence and abuse. A counselor without knowledge of domestic violence will not be able to understand or assist you effectively in your emotional healing. A support group dealing with issues other than domestic violence will not be able to offer the support you need to stay free. Most areas have a local YWCA or women's shelter that offers a battered women's support group, which will be invaluable to your healing. Again, prequalify your support team by making sure they're educated in the field of domestic violence and abuse.

In these meditations, I most often use the term *she* for the abused and *he* for the abuser. Please substitute the pronouns that best fit your own situation. Abuse occurs in many types of relationships, and the abuser can be of either gender. Remind yourself, as you remain free, to look at the similarities between your own situation and others' rather than focus on any differences. Many domestic violence situations have their own unique characteristics, but the dynamics of domestic violence remain the same throughout the world. Domestic violence is about power and control, period.

I congratulate and honor you for your courage and determination in taking back your life and for making the effort to fly free. May you find the peace your life has been missing and the strength to move forward with each passing day. My wish is for you to discover the song in your heart that's been silenced or compose a new one that's louder and more beautiful than you could ever have imagined. May you find the knowledge that you are worthy of kindness and the ambition to accomplish your goals. May you discover your wings of independence and soar higher than you ever believed possible.

Important note: If you've recently left or are thinking of leaving an abusive relationship, you might begin your healing process by reading my first book, *Time to Break Free: Meditations for the First 100 Days After Leaving an Abusive Relationship.*

➤ *Day 1*

I have accomplished something of great significance. I decided to break free from an abusive relationship, and I did it. Now it's time to make another decision, the decision to fly free. Today I will make a commitment to myself to stay on my path of freedom and learn how to further develop the skills that will change my life. Being free from abuse has already changed my life for the better, and now I will begin to make it better than it's ever been.

➤ Day 2

Today I will write five things that I would like others to say about or directly to me. They can be sentences or words that sound comforting, supportive, or flattering. Even if I don't believe the statements right now, I will write five positive things that I would like others to think about me. Sometimes people might say things that make me feel uncomfortable or hurt, but as I make my list, I'll become more aware of compliments I would like to hear.

➤ *Day 3*

Today I will look at my list from yesterday and choose my favorite statement. Then I'll rewrite the statement using *I* instead of *you*. If the statement is directed *to* me, I change it to be *about* me. If I've written a one-word compliment, I'll put it after "I am. . ." For example, "I love you" becomes "I am loved," and "she is courageous" becomes "I am courageous." If I can't choose just one statement, I will combine them into one sentence, such as "I am loved and I am courageous." I will say this sentence ten times in the morning and ten times in the evening each day on twenty-one days. To live without abuse is to change something that became familiar, and I'm proud of myself for making such a serious effort to do so.

➤ *Day 4*

Today I will promise myself that I will have no contact with my abuser. I can't move forward in my healing and truly recover while I'm still in contact or having a relationship with the person who has abused me. If there are child custody matters, I will do whatever I can to find someone else to help me avoid contact. Perhaps a mediator, family member, friend, advocate, or court-appointed supervisor could help me convey necessary information to my abuser. I will not engage in unnecessary phone conversations or meet him at his request. I'm committed to breaking free of my abuser's hold on me, and the best way to do this is to begin by having no contact. In addition, I will say my favorite sentence out loud ten times, twice a day.

I know that I want a good and secure life. I believe that I deserve one. Today I will remind myself of all the right choices I'm making to have one. My abuser may have been the "provider" in our household and used that position to control me. I can get help in supporting myself and my children. I can get financial assistance, get job training, get an education, or develop a plan for my income. I will believe that I can earn a living without my abuser. I refuse to believe my abuser's statement that I couldn't make it without him. I will believe that I can earn a living or set goals that will help me earn a living on my own. In addition, I will say my favorite sentence out loud ten times, twice a day.

➤ *Day 6*

My abuser might have emotionally abused me by telling me he was superior. My abuser might have told me that I was stupid, incompetent, or illiterate; that I couldn't make it on my own, wasn't good for anything, or could never get a job. Today I will realize that I'm smart enough to ask for help and that I don't have to depend on an abusive person. I don't have to depend on anyone who doesn't treat me the way I deserve to be treated. I deserve love, respect, and to have others listen to what I say. In addition, I will say my favorite sentence out loud ten times, twice a day.

➤ Day 7

If I have to speak to my abuser, or any abuser, I will refrain from falling into old behavior. Old behavior is anything I might say or do that reminds me of arguments or feelings from the past. In current conversations, I will react differently. If my abuser says things that used to upset or anger me, I can use a different response. If I have to speak to my abuser on the phone, and he becomes critical or angry, I can say, "If you continue to talk to me this way, I will have to hang up." My abuser and I might have been reacting to each other in the same way for a long time. Today I will change the way I speak to him and break free of old communication patterns. I don't have to use a tone of voice or language that reminds me of the past. If I can't think of new responses, I can choose to say nothing for now. If it's difficult to think of new ways of speaking or new things to say, I will make a list of things to say next time. It's important to learn new patterns of communication if I'm to get through this time of emotional healing and grow as a person. In addition, I will say my favorite sentence out loud ten times, twice a day.

➤ *Day 8*

If I've not been writing in a journal, I will begin today. If I'm already writing in a journal, I will try writing about my feelings in more detail. I can write about the day's events, how I felt when they happened, what I would like to change about them, or how I'm feeling in general. I will remind myself how important it is to write about my feelings and thoughts, see them on paper, and fully process them. I will keep my journal in a safe place and continue to write in it each day as an important part of my healing. In addition, I will say my favorite sentence out loud ten times, twice a day.

➤ *Day 9*

Today I will pay attention to little things that bother me, and I'll begin to realize when I want them to stop. Whether they are loud noises or sounds, loud or offensive talking, traffic, or even bright light, I'll become more aware of things that annoy me and when I want them to stop. Once I'm aware of this, I can take action. Whenever possible, I will turn down the TV or radio, ask someone to speak more quietly, or take a different road on the way to work. If I can't stop whatever is bothering me, I will at least feel grateful for my increased awareness. I used to block out or ignore such things, but I'm becoming more aware each day of what is acceptable in my life and what is not. In addition, I will say my favorite sentence out loud ten times, twice a day.

➤ *Day 10*

I'm becoming much better at staying focused. I realize that I don't mentally escape or "zone out" as much as I used to when I'm listening to someone talk or watching a television program. I'm learning how to tune in to my own life. I pay attention to the sounds, smells, colors, and images in my life. Even a painful moment or situation, in which I'm reminded of my past abuse, only shows me that I'm more tuned in to my life now. I feel confident that I've grown, that I'm healing and getting stronger. In addition, I will say my favorite sentence out loud ten times, twice a day.

Loneliness can sneak up on me when I least expect it. I might not feel comfortable in my loneliness, but it doesn't mean I have to fix it by contacting my abuser or seeking out another intimate relationship. I have other options, and today I will practice them. I will find something else to do with my time, such as read a book or story, write, rent a movie, go for a walk, or spend time with my children. I can think about things I've always wanted to do, and I can begin doing them. I can simply experience the loneliness itself and allow myself to be alone. There's a difference between feeling lonely and being alone. Learning how to spend time by myself is a good thing. Even though I may have felt isolated in my old relationship, I can enjoy being alone without feeling isolated. In addition, I will say my favorite sentence out loud ten times, twice a day.

➤ *Day 12*

Are there parts of my past that I've refused to think about? Are there feelings I've put aside for later? Are there situations or memories that I couldn't face before? I'm stronger in my healing, and I can now look at things with more awareness, confidence, and perspective. I can begin to look at the parts of my past that were difficult to think about or admit before. I can talk about them with my therapist or counselor. I can write in my journal about events that have caused me pain, remembering that I'm not willing to be part of an abusive relationship anymore. I can begin to deal with the painful thoughts that I couldn't face before. In addition, I will say my favorite sentence out loud ten times, twice a day.

➤ *Day 13*

Today I will practice letting go of shame. Am I feeling guilty for having been in an abusive relationship? Do I keep telling myself that I should have done things differently? Do I often feel overwhelmed with guilt for having exposed myself and my children to such frightening behavior? Do I feel sad or depressed or dislike myself? Today I will begin a new way of thinking about my past. I will understand that there were many reasons why I stayed. Eventually I will be able to better understand them, but I don't have to name them or understand them right now. I can simply remind myself that I did the best I could at the time. This may be difficult, especially when other family members or friends are questioning me. I don't have to be interrogated or questioned. I can ask them to stop, letting them know that I'm aware of what happened and that I'm seeking help. I can ask them to be patient and to stop asking me for information that I'm not ready to give. I will find comfort in knowing that even though I may have made mistakes, I'm learning from them now and moving forward in a positive direction.

Today I will continue to practice balance. If I spend most of my time with my children, I will plan something with another adult or friend. If I spend most of my time working, I will plan something fun. I need to have a mix of different activities in my life so that I can enjoy it to the fullest. If the scales are tipped on one side, I will make a commitment to balance them out. Today I will plan to do one new activity that creates a greater balance in my life. In addition, I will say my favorite sentence out loud ten times, twice a day.

➤ *Day 15*

Today I will take care of my health. I might need to start eating regularly or eating a better diet. If I'm experiencing health problems because of the abuse I've endured, I will seek professional help. If I've sustained injuries that require attention, I will make an appointment to see a doctor, dentist, or chiropractor. Perhaps I experience headaches or pain that should not be ignored. If I've been eating poorly, I can read about good nutrition or take vitamins. I might benefit from a massage or day at a spa. Along with healing my mind, I need to heal my body. Today I will pay attention to what my body needs and find solutions. In addition, I will say my favorite sentence out loud ten times, twice a day.

➤ *Day 16*

Today I will buy a helium balloon. I'll take it to a place that is meaningful or peaceful to me. I'll imagine my abuser inside the balloon, and I'll let it go. As I watch it float upward, I'll say good-bye, scream at it, laugh, cry, or allow any other emotion that comes to the surface. I'm willing to let go of the feelings about my abuser that are not good for me. Even if I'm not quite ready to let my abuser go completely, I'll watch the balloon until I can't see it anymore. Day by day, bit by bit, I will continue to let go. In addition, I will say my favorite sentence out loud ten times, twice a day.

➤ Day 17

When friends or others tell me about their hard times or problems, I will be aware of how much I can handle. If their problems become too much for me, I can gently ask them to stop sharing them with me. I can let them know that I'm feeling vulnerable at this time in my life, and I need to take care of myself first. Becoming too involved in the problems of others can prevent me from moving forward in my own healing. Today I will know the difference between being a compassionate friend and being codependent or taking on too much responsibility. I will take care of myself and my children before helping others. In addition, I will say my favorite sentence out loud ten times, twice a day.

➤ Day 18

With each day that passes, I will remind myself that I'm doing the right thing. At times it might feel like I should have done things differently in the past. Maybe I wish I'd stayed longer or given my abuser another chance. I might wonder whether our relationship would have worked out if I'd only stayed a little longer. I don't have to spend as much time wondering as I used to. I can quickly remind myself that I've made the right choice, and I'm making the right choices now. I did the best I could do, and I'm doing the best I can. I can move forward in my healing each day. I have survived so much and come so far in my progress. I'm one of the bravest people I know. In addition, I will say my favorite sentence out loud ten times, twice a day.

➤ Day 19

There are days when I might miss the company of my abuser. It's important for me to realize that what I'm probably missing is companionship, not my abuser. Perhaps there are only parts of the relationship I miss. There were probably some good times that I wish I could still experience in my life. On these days I will remember the pain, the aching feeling inside, the fear, and the desperation I felt. I can have companionship without everything else that comes with being abused. I deserve companionship that makes me feel peaceful, happy, and fulfilled. I will remind myself that I will eventually have it with someone who won't abuse me. In addition, I will say my favorite sentence out loud ten times, twice a day.

My abuser might be trying to win me back or want me to be a friend. He might have tried to regain my trust or promised to change. But since I left, has my abuser been in counseling? Has my abuser been through an extensive anger-diversion program? Has he made genuine efforts to change? If so, I can be glad for him, but it doesn't mean I should go back. If reconciliation is something I really want, I won't even consider it unless I have positive proof, including professional opinions, that major change has occurred for at least six months. I will watch and listen for any signs of abusive behavior. Does he try to control me in any way? Does he offer too many suggestions or ask too many questions? Does he tell me what to do without my asking for his opinion? I'll pay attention to these signs not only in my abuser, but in any relationship. I'm working hard at staying free of abusive people, and these signs help me to do so. If it's difficult for me to keep track of warning signs, I can keep a journal or a list of specific statements or incidents. I can see how much my abuser has changed, if at all, and make a more informed decision.

➤ *Day 21*

My children still need my help. They have been through a lot, and I need to reassure them that I'm learning and growing. I need to let them know that I made some choices in the past that were not good for me or for us, but I'm making better choices now. Their trust in me was affected, but it comforts me to know that I'm working on earning it back. I will promise my children that I will do everything I can to keep them and myself safe. I will also make this promise to myself. In addition, I will say my favorite sentence out loud ten times, twice a day.

➤ Day 22

Today I will be aware of people around me who try to minimize my feelings or my situation. Phrases like "it's not that bad" or "you're making a big deal out of nothing" or "don't be so sensitive" only make me feel that I'm wrong. I'm not wrong in any feeling that I might have. Even though my perception of a situation may not be accurate, my feelings about it are not wrong. When others minimize how I'm feeling or reacting, they're basically telling me that I don't deserve to feel the way I do or that I should feel differently. I deserve to feel the way I do, and I don't have to change my feelings to please others. I'm not making a big deal out of nothing, because if I'm having feelings, they're obviously about something. I'm not too sensitive, because I'm reacting in ways that feel right for me. When others try to minimize my situation, they don't validate me or my emotions. When I don't feel heard or validated, it perpetuates my old feelings of being abused and having done something wrong. Today I will remind myself that my feelings aren't and can't be wrong. I have the right to whatever feelings I may have and to have people around me who care enough to listen without criticizing.

Today I will look for and cut out pictures of things I want in my life or things I want to experience. Magazines or catalogs are good places to look. The things I want can be objects, feelings, concepts, goals, words, or statements. Even if they seem to be out of reach now, I will cut them out. I will paste them on cardboard or posterboard, or inside a photo album. I can write little notes or sayings beside them that mean something special to me. I will make a game of it, something that I can enjoy. I can add to my collection whenever I want and hang it in my room to look at every day. All that I see, all that I want, all that I hope for is possible. I like being able to see where I want to be in my life. In addition, I will say my favorite sentence out loud ten times, twice a day.

➤ *Day 24*

Before I get out of bed each morning, I will get a clear picture of my life in my mind. I will feel gratitude for the absence of abuse, and I'll remind myself that my life is getting better with each day. This doesn't mean that something great needs to happen every day. It doesn't mean that I measure my success by how far I progress every day. It means that my life is better with each passing day—with each passing minute—because I choose to accept kindness instead of abuse. I choose to be nurtured instead of belittled, loved instead of beaten, supported instead of criticized, and listened to instead of ignored. Even when I face life's problems, they are easier than the gigantic problem of being abused. I will thank myself for making such a courageous decision to break free, stay free, and fly free. In addition, I will say my favorite sentence out loud ten times, twice a day.

My perception of danger may have been distorted by the abuse I've lived with in the past. I might not be as afraid or as cautious as I should be or need to be in certain situations. On the other hand, I might be overly sensitive to danger and overreact. While I pay attention to my own feelings, I realize I might also need to depend on others for their opinions of what is dangerous, at least until my own perception becomes more accurate. My abuser might have clouded my thinking by telling me that I was imagining danger or by saying, "It's all in your mind." I might have believed him and let it affect my way of thinking. If I'm not sure whether a situation or person is dangerous, I will ask the opinion of my therapist, my support group facilitator, or a close friend whom I know I can trust. In addition, I will say my favorite sentence out loud ten times, twice a day.

I will begin to pay attention to my own intuition when deciding whether certain individuals are safe for me to be around. Do they say things that remind me of my abuser? Do they act in ways, even if not very often, that remind me of my abuser? Do I get a funny feeling around them? Even if I can't really pinpoint what it might be, I can be aware when something doesn't seem quite right. I can pay attention to the little voice inside that might be trying to warn me. I will be cautious and observant. I will watch and listen carefully to see if my uneasy feeling continues. I don't have to be around or be friends with someone who sets off warning signals, whatever they might be. I will not ignore the signs, and I will not make excuses for them. I won't tell myself that they're only in my head or only figments of my imagination. I will pay attention to times when I don't feel comfortable with someone. I can pay more attention to my intuition and develop it as part of my healing. It is a good thing, and it can help keep me safe. In addition, I will say my favorite sentence out loud ten times, twice a day.

Today I will say my favorite sentence out loud ten times, twice a day. This is the twenty-first day of saying my favorite sentence. I can feel the difference. I can feel the comfort and support I've given to myself. Whether or not other people say things I want to hear, I can say them to myself and believe they're true. I don't have to wait for acceptance or compliments from others. I am courageous, I am brave, I am willing, I am good. I deserve to be happy; I deserve a good life. I deserve to feel and be safe. If I so desire, I can choose another phrase to say to myself for another twenty-one days.

➤ *Day 28*

Have I taken care of any legal work that needs to be done? Have I filed for custody of my children? Do I have my restraining order? Is it current? Do I need to file for a divorce? Today I will contemplate the legal matters in my life and take care of what I need to do. It might be that I need to make phone calls and find legal representation with which I feel comfortable. Perhaps I need to look on the Internet and read about the laws that apply to me in my state or country. Maybe I need to find out if I qualify for victim's assistance or call local women's assistance programs to see what help is available. Even though I might not want to tackle this now, it's important for me to do so. Being responsible with legalities is part of being independent and keeping myself and my children safe.

➤ *Day 29*

Today I will be aware of old thought or behavior patterns. If I see someone out in public whom I find attractive, I might suddenly realize that he fits the picture of past intimate, abusive partners. I might find myself drawn to relationships with people who are similar to those who have abused me, treated me badly, or made me feel uncomfortable. I will recognize this pattern and begin to realize when I'm falling back into it. I don't have to criticize myself for feeling this way. It's okay to take a few steps backward as long as I'm aware of it and get back on track. I can remind myself that this is a past behavior or an old desire that I no longer need in my life. I can then move forward into what I want now. This process doesn't take as long as it used to. In the past I might have thought about pursuing such a desire for weeks or even months. Now I might think about it for only a matter of minutes, or it might be a fleeting thought that lasts a few seconds. Realizing this, I feel confident that I'm going in the right direction and growing stronger each day.

➤ *Day 30*

Today I will imagine the color of my feelings. I can use paper and colored pencils, markers, crayons, or paints for my project. Using color and without drawing any specific image, I will make a picture of anger. What color is anger? What shape is it? Does it have sharp edges, or is it smooth? Do I color it quickly or slowly? Is anger small or large? How do I feel while I'm creating this image? Am I thinking about what I'm doing or simply allowing myself to feel? When I've finished my picture of anger, I may choose to make separate pictures of other feelings, such as sadness, fear, surprise, joy, excitement, or others that have special meaning to me. This project can put me in touch with the simplicity of my emotions instead of the words and thoughts my mind usually attaches to them. I don't have to be an artist to do this project, nor do I have to show it to anyone else. It's also a project that my children and I can do together. There is no need to analyze each picture with them; I will simply allow them to express themselves using the colors of their choice. If they want to talk about their pictures, I will simply listen. If they choose not to discuss them with me, I will respect their privacy.

➤ *Day 31*

Being abused wasn't my fault. I didn't do anything wrong to deserve it, and I did the best I could given the situation. Today I will notice the things for which I *am* responsible. I'm responsible for obeying the law, being a safe driver, paying my bills, doing my dishes, washing my clothes, and many other things. When something is my responsibility and I don't attend to it, then the consequences *are* my fault and no one else's. Being a free and independent person means that I take responsibility for certain things in my life. Today I will make a list of all the things for which I'm responsible.

➤ *Day 32*

Today I will look at my list of responsibilities. Is it overwhelming? If so, is there someone I could ask for temporary help? Is there something on the list that doesn't have to be there? Is there some way I could simplify my list? Perhaps I could make a shorter list of things to be done before lunch and another list of things to be done before dinner. I could make a list of things I have to do only once a week or once a month. Looking at several smaller lists can be less overwhelming than one long one. I used to think it would be impossible to be on my own. I'm discovering that while it may be difficult, it's not impossible. Making lists helps keep things in perspective so I don't get overwhelmed. Completing my list helps me feel a sense of accomplishment. I can finish what I start, and I can complete tasks that need to be done. I can depend on me.

➤ *Day 33*

Today I will make a list of what I've achieved since I left my abuser. Do I have my own place? Do I take good care of my children? Do I have a job that I like or one with which I can pay the bills on my own? Am I happy? Am I comfortable spending time with people who aren't abusive? Have I gone back to school? Have I learned a new skill? Have I received a promotion at work? Do I make my own decisions? Wherever I am in my life, I will notice where I am compared to where I came from. It is often easy to take positive changes for granted or let them go unnoticed. But today I'll list all the things I've been able to do without someone else controlling me or hurting me. Today I will be satisfied and proud to be where I am right now.

➤ *Day 34*

Today, when I look at a tree, I will look not only at the branches but also at the space in between them. When I look at a window, I'll see the frame and then look at the shape of the glass inside. When I look at an object, I'll look at its image and then notice the shape of its shadow. When I look in the mirror, I'll see my face and the shape of the space around it. Today I will start viewing things in a different way. This technique can help me increase my awareness and my perception of my surroundings. Things might not always be what they appear to be. There's usually more than one way to look at a situation or problem. Today I will look at the shapes that surround the obvious and practice noticing what I usually don't see. By doing this exercise, I'm opening my mind and increasing my awareness to new ways of thinking.

When young children are first learning to read, they begin with the basics. After learning the alphabet and the sound that each letter makes, they put them together to form the simplest of words, then short sentences. In my life without abuse, my healing process may be similar. My leaving was comparable to a child becoming willing to read. Learning about the dynamics of domestic violence and how they relate to my own situation is like learning my alphabet. Once I begin to implement suggestions and advice from people who are knowledgeable about domestic violence, I'll learn how to put the letters of my life together to make words. Soon, I will have enough information to begin a life without abuse and make decisions that will keep me out of abusive relationships. I don't have to be upset that I'm not farther along than I want to be. When children are first beginning to read, they read slowly and make mistakes. Today I will allow myself the same consideration and patience. Before long, I will be able to make wise decisions quickly, but for now, as long as I'm willing to learn, I will be patient with myself.

➤ *Day 36*

Today I will do one thing that I felt I couldn't do before because it would have upset my abuser. Perhaps it's trying a new hairstyle or hair color. It might be wearing my makeup differently or buying an outfit that I know he wouldn't have liked. I can change the way I arrange the furniture, or I may choose to hang pictures that I like but know my abuser wouldn't have appreciated. I can make my own choices about the way things look and happen in my life. I will continually practice making my own choices and decisions.

Today I will live without trying to win the approval of others. As I look back on my relationships, do I notice that it was important for me to have others' approval? Did my actions revolve around trying to get people to like me, or did I do whatever was necessary to feel appreciated? Perhaps the challenge of gaining approval was more important to me than actually having those people in my life. Maybe the attraction was to see whether I could make that person like me or fall in love with me. It's possible that this behavior began when I was young and trying to gain the approval of a parent. I might have felt so rejected or unloved that I believed I had to try as hard as I could to win love and acceptance. Today I will remind myself that no matter how I felt when I was young, I no longer have to try to win over others by changing who I am. I deserve to meet people who will like me, and love me, for who I am now and not for what I do to please them. I don't need to be overly generous, kind, or good to manipulate others into liking me. When I'm genuine and honest about who I am, I'm rewarded with lasting, quality relationships.

➤ Day 38

Today I will buy and prepare food that I want to eat. If I want to try a certain diet, eat healthier food, or learn a new way of cooking, I will. I can choose the food I want to eat without asking someone else's permission. If I have children, I will encourage them to try new things too, and let them help me shop for different meals. I can also ask my children to help prepare the meals, and we can enjoy expanding our food preferences together. If I find that my children refuse to eat something new, I can still make it for myself. I deserve to eat the things I want to eat without always having to please others.

➤ Day 39

Today I will focus on communication with my children. I will make a commitment to talk with them each day by making a game of it. I'll teach them "The Sharing Game." At the end of the day, we each take turns sharing the following:

1. What made me the happiest today?
2. What made me the saddest today?
3. What made me the angriest today?
4. What made me feel the safest today?

This game allows us to remember different experiences throughout the day and how we felt about them. Experiences that bring happiness or sadness are not always the same for everyone. By playing this game, my children and I are getting to know each other better as individuals. If I don't have children, I will ask these questions for myself.

➤ *Day 40*

In addition to writing in my journal each day, I'll add a new daily ritual today. Before going to bed, I will think of one word that represents my day. I'll choose only one word. I'll make a picture of the word, write it down on a "sticky" note, write it in my journal, add it to my picture collage, or begin a new collage of words. Each day I can look in a dictionary, thesaurus, library, or other place to find the words I need or to learn new words that best represent my day. On doing this exercise, I am learning how to make decisions by choosing one word instead of several. I'm learning how to choose the things I like best and make choices that appeal to me. I'm also learning how to simplify my life. When thinking or speaking about certain events, I might get wrapped up in the details and drama, not knowing when to stop. When I can choose one word that best describes my day, I'm learning how to stop myself from endlessly talking, being overly dramatic, or obsessing in my mind. I will learn how to simplify my life, the way I think of it, and how I speak of it.

I'm working hard to fly free of abuse. I know that each day is another day of freedom, and I savor each one. Even though I have responsibilities, difficult times, and struggles with being on my own, I'm happy to be free of abuse; this freedom was my hope for a long time. Today I will find a box or container that is special to me. I can call it my God box or goal box, or whatever name I choose. I will write my goals on slips of paper and put them inside. Each time I meet one of these goals, I can take it out and feel proud of myself for being able to set goals and achieve them. What a strong and courageous person I am!

➤ *Day 42*

Today I will pay attention to how I speak to others. Do I use words that describe how I feel, or do I accuse others of making me feel a certain way? Do I take responsibility for my own feelings? Do I understand that I'm the one who chooses how I feel? Do I express myself in ways that are understandable? Am I clear about what I want to say? Do I express myself accurately, or do people have to guess what I mean? I can be honest about my thoughts and feelings. If I'm afraid of hurting someone's feelings, I can say what I mean without being mean. I will learn how to speak to others without hurting them and be honest at the same time.

Today I will accept all aspects of my life. Have I recently felt discouraged? Are my expectations too high regarding what I want to achieve and how quickly I think it should happen? Have I set too many goals or do I want to accomplish them in an unreasonable amount of time? Just because I didn't get something or somewhere as quickly as I wanted to doesn't mean I won't. If meeting a specific goal seems to be a struggle or constant battle, perhaps it's something I don't really need to achieve yet. Maybe I need to practice a little patience instead of trying to force things to happen so quickly. I can reevaluate my ambitions and decide which of them is most important to me. Which goals do I really want to accomplish, and which ones are causing me problems? I'm happy that I can make plans in my own life, but I don't have to be so hard on myself when things don't go the way I had planned. Today I accept the fact that I might not always succeed in everything I set out to do. I can choose what is most important and focus on one or two goals at a time. I may find that by simplifying my life, I feel more successful and less defeated.

Today I will take a moment to think of all those who are still in abusive relationships. I've been lucky, or blessed, that I was able to leave my abuser. Other people might not be where I am, and they might not even be interested in being where I am. I can think of them today and feel sorry for their pain. I can grieve for the children in those situations who might never recover and for their mothers—or fathers—who don't realize they have options. I can say a prayer for them, make a donation to a local shelter, or put a note about them in my God box or goal box. When I write something down and place it inside the box, I'm turning it over to God, my Spiritual Power, or whatever I choose to call my spiritual beliefs. I'm able to let it go, knowing that I can't fix everything or take care of everyone. When I think of all the people who are still in abusive relationships, I can be compassionate about what they must be going through and, at the same time, be grateful for how far I've come in my own life. Today I will say a little prayer to my Spiritual Power: Thank you, thank you, thank you for showing me the way to freedom.

I might have a difficult time during holidays, especially holidays that focus on couples. Any holiday can be depressing if I'm feeling lonely or wishing things could be different. Perhaps holidays represent being together with family, and my idea of what that means is different from the way my life is now. I can create new traditions and new ways of celebrating without feeling that I've no reason to enjoy holidays. I can create celebrations that might be different from what I experienced in the past, new ways of enjoying special days for myself and for my children. I don't have to be stuck in old ways of celebrating but can find other ways of making memories for us. When it comes to holidays or special days like Valentine's Day, I don't need to feel depressed that I'm no longer part of a couple. Valentine's Day is simply a day to celebrate love, and I can celebrate the fact that I love myself. I don't need someone else to validate me. I can buy myself flowers, a gift, candy, or a card. I can remind myself that the most important person in my life is me. I can send valentines to friends, co-workers, or my children. I don't have to be part of a couple to enjoy the celebration of love.

Today I will start to recognize "red flags." Red flags are signals, that little feeling in the pit of my stomach, something that goes against what I know to be true or causes me to feel uncomfortable. Red flags come in all sizes. They can be small and quite subtle or very large and obvious. If I've told someone I'm dating that I have plans for the evening, but he still shows up with a dozen roses, it's a little red flag. On the outside, it might seem a sweet gesture, especially if he claims that he missed me and couldn't stay away. If he refuses to leave, that's a big red flag. Whether the flag is large or small, the important thing is that this person is not respecting my boundaries. Ignoring boundaries is similar to ridiculously believing that "when women say no, they really mean yes." If this person can't respect a simple boundary about my plans for the evening, what will he do with a boundary that's more significant? In the past, I probably saw red flags and ignored them. Today all I have to do is decide how many red flags need to be raised before I realize a relationship is a bad idea. A well-known baseball rule works well: three strikes and you're out.

It's okay for me to feel angry. I've been hurt by someone I know and cared about, and I didn't like it. That person acted with violence or manipulation when he was angry or even most of the time. I can be aware of and feel my own anger, but I can choose to show it in different ways than he did. I can hit a pillow or scream in the car. I can draw pictures of how I feel, using the color that best represents my anger. I can write angry letters to my abuser that I won't send. I can think of different and safe ways to express myself without hurting others. I can tell someone that I'm angry and give the reasons why by talking to him or her in a quiet, reasonable way. I don't have to hit or verbally abuse other people when I'm angry. I can be a better person by experiencing and expressing my anger in appropriate ways.

➤ Day 48

Some days I might not be able to stop thinking about every detail in my life. It seems as though I can't stop all the analyzing, processing, trying to understand, resolving, or blaming. It is during these times that I need to "get out of my head" and do something physically active. I can wash the car, clean out the cupboards, scrub the floors, clean out a closet, clean under the sink, hose down the driveway, take part in a sports activity, or simply pull weeds in the yard. Getting out of my head and getting my body busy helps me let go of thoughts that keep spinning around in my mind. I might have to force myself to get up and do something physical, but today or whenever I feel like this, I will give my mind a break and let my body be busy.

If I'm worried about problems or issues in my life, I will create a "worry wall." I will find a blank wall and write each thing I'm worried about on a separate "sticky" note or index card. I will then attach them to the wall, their height depending on the degree to which I worry about them. The higher I put the note on the wall, the more I'm worried about it. The lower I place the note, the less I'm worried about it. Each day I will review my worry wall and adjust my worries. Have some worries become more intense? Have some of the problems been solved? Have some of my worries become smaller? This exercise gives me the opportunity to actually look at my worries and visually review them daily rather than keeping them all in my mind. I will notice how long it takes each of my worries to be resolved, and then I'll decide if my worrying about them affected the outcome. I might even suggest that my older children do the same.

➤ *Day 50*

Today I will remember to breathe deeply. When I'm upset about a problem or situation, I will notice how I'm breathing. Am I holding my breath? Am I short of breath? Am I breathing rapidly? Every time I get anxious or upset, I will remember to take ten slow, deep breaths. This technique can be calming and will help me deal with the problem or situation in a more reasonable way. I may even find that, during intense situations, it's helpful to leave the room to practice my deep breathing. My awareness of my feelings is valuable, and so is teaching my body and my mind to work together.

I know how to deal with fear and worry using various tools; however, some situations require more. If someone has been threatening me, stalking me, obsessing over me, or harassing me, I need to do more than write about it in my journal or place a note on my worry wall. These matters are serious and may require me to file a report with the police, get a restraining order, or get a security system. I might need to take a class on self-defense or find another place to stay. Most domestic violence homicides occur after the victim leaves the relationship. If I suspect that I'm in danger, I will take appropriate measures to ensure the safety of myself and my children. I will not take serious threats lightly. I will not rationalize a dangerous situation. I will pay attention to signs, red flags, and my intuition. I will pay attention to my surroundings and practice perception, looking for signs that indicate something might happen. My perception of danger has probably been so distorted that I'm not sure what real danger is or how to recognize its potential. If I'm uncertain, I can call a hot line or talk to a police officer, women's advocate, or violence specialist. I've learned to use many tools to ensure my emotional safety. Today I will begin to ensure my physical safety.

➤ Day 52

Today I will take a break if I need one. If I'm tired, I will find time to rest or take a nap. When regular daily tasks or chores become exhausting, I will remember to take time to relax, even if only for a few minutes. If I have children, perhaps I can rest with them instead of using their rest time to finish my work. Housework can be done at any time, and there are times when I feel like doing nothing. If I'm at work, I can rest in my car or sit outside during my break. As long as I'm not procrastinating or manipulating others to take care of my responsibilities, I can create my own work schedule. I will remember that my well-being and the well-being of my children come first. I can't move forward in my healing if I'm overly tired or overworked.

➤ Day 53

Today I will notice the positive ways other people treat each other. Wherever I go, I will pay attention to the behavior of others and become more in touch with behaviors I want in my life. Do I see a parent holding hands with a child? Do I ever hold hands with my children? Do I wish I did it more often? Do I see a couple embracing or kissing? Is that something I want in my life? Do I see families picnicking in the park? Is that something I want to do with my children? Do I hear someone give a friend a compliment? Is that the way I want to speak to others or have others speak to me? Do I notice people smiling at each other or saying good morning? I will notice the people around me and start to imitate the behavior I like. Perhaps I never learned to be affectionate or never believed it was appropriate. Perhaps no one ever showed me the kindness I see in others. I might not have learned loving or positive ways of communicating or interacting with others, and they might seem unfamiliar to me. I'm willing to learn new behaviors, however, and I'll begin by practicing them daily.

➤ Day 54

I know that I've experienced the cycle of violence, but today I will be aware that healthy relationships work in cycles too. Instead of a tension-building phase before conflict occurs, healthy relationships might have a build-up phase. The people involved might realize that a problem has arisen. There is an awareness that something is about to happen: a confrontation, a debate, an argument, or a need to express feelings. When the tension reaches a crucial point, feelings are aired and a confrontation might take place, but in a nonviolent way. I can learn the difference between the tension-building phase and the build-up phase. I can be aware that people who aren't abusive can still be angry, and when that happens I don't have to fear for my safety. When I have friends who aren't abusive, I can accept my own mistakes or misunderstandings without fear of violence. I can learn ways of participating in this phase even though it's new to me. I can experience the anticipation of a confrontation or disagreement without fear. People who aren't abusive express their feelings all the time without hitting, breaking things, or hurting others.

In the cycle of violence, the second phase is the acute battering incident. In healthy relationships, it may simply be called a confrontation. During this phase, people may be expressing their feelings or emotions; communicating their disappointment, dislikes, and anger; or setting their boundaries. There is no hitting, battering, name-calling, or violence. Healthy, nurturing relationships don't contain abusive behavior. Today I will learn the difference between the acute battering incident and a confrontation. I can confront and express myself with healthy-minded people without fear of being hit. I can express my feelings to healthy-minded people without fear of them leaving my life. I can tell a healthy-minded person that I feel angry without the fear of being yelled at. I realize this type of communication is new for me and may take some time to learn. I might still feel afraid during a confrontation, but I will realize that it's only because it reminds me of my past.

In the cycle of violence, the third phase is called the honeymoon phase. In healthy relationships this phase may be simply be called closure. Closure occurs when feelings have been expressed and heard. There might be apologies, and forgiveness might be offered. There might be relief or a feeling of validation. If the people in the confrontation arrive at agreement, there might be laughing, affection, or a deeper level of intimacy. A couple might even have sex afterward. In a healthy relationship, there is mutual understanding and real closeness, not the distorted sense of closeness found in an abusive and controlling relationship. After a violent confrontation, I may have had sex with my abuser out of fear, in hopes that things would change, or because I was forced to. In a healthy relationship, if I choose to have sex after a confrontation, it's because I want to feel close after reaching some kind of closure or agreement. Today I will realize the difference between the honeymoon phase and closure. I can feel relieved and at peace after a healthy confrontation. I will also notice that if a confrontation occurs, and the other person displays abusive behavior, it's not a relationship that I want in my life.

Have I been using alcohol or drugs since I left my abuser? Do I use them to "take the edge off" or to numb my pain? Have I wondered if I have a problem with alcohol or substance abuse? Have I thought about stopping? Is it affecting relationships with my children or other people I care about? If I answer yes to any of these questions, I will find out more about alcoholism or addiction. Alcohol or drugs won't make my problems go away, and they won't help me get through my healing process any faster or easier. I will merely be adding another problem to my life. Today I will seriously consider whether or not I have this problem. If I'm not sure, then I probably need to find out. I can attend Twelve Step meetings or read literature on the subject. Am I taking prescription medication? Does my doctor know about my history of being abused? I might want to seek a second opinion about any medications I'm taking. I want to stay free of any kind of abuse, including substance or alcohol abuse.

➤ *Day 58*

Today I will look at the relationships I have in my life now. Are there any that are abusive? Are there relationships that feel uncomfortable? Are there people in my life whom I don't like? If I still have abusive relationships in my life, I will consider ending them. If these relationships are with friends, I can tell them that we no longer have anything in common. If they're with family members, I can choose to spend less time with them. I don't have to attend gatherings or events just to please others, and I can decline an invitation that doesn't interest me. I don't have to participate in relationships that don't fit into the plan I have for my life. I have the right to stay away from people who don't treat me the way I deserve to be treated.

Today I will appreciate my courage. I will remind myself how bad I used to feel, how most of my behavior and decisions were guided by someone else, how I made excuses for everything that was happening to me, and how I used to think it was my fault. Today I can appreciate how far I've come in my healing. Today I will slow down and take time to appreciate what I've already done. I will look in the rearview mirror of my life and feel grateful that the abuse is in the past. The road hasn't always been smooth, but I remember how dangerous it was then, and I appreciate how far I've traveled. I am an example of success. I am worthy of praise. I am a winner, and the prize is my new life.

➤ *Day 60*

Have I run across old pictures of my abuser, old letters, poems, or personal items of his? Today I will decide what to do with them. Depending on the circumstances, I may choose to save them for my children or ask them if they want to keep these items. I might even ask them to keep the items in their own room or in a drawer. If these items are reminders of something I don't want to forget, is there a reason for me to remember it? Were the good times really that good? Or were they good only in comparison to everything else? If there is no reason to keep these things, I can throw them away, tear them up, burn them, or bury them. I don't have to keep reminders of my abuser. Today I will begin to clean out my life.

Today I will let go of the fantasy I created around my abusive relationship. If I could have the relationship I've always wanted, what would it look like? What things would my partner and I do together? What would our lives be like? When I have this picture clearly in my mind, I will ask myself, "Does my abuser, or the person I'm involved with now, fit into this picture?" Today I will realize that the relationship I want for myself and my children didn't and doesn't include being abused. Today I will say good-bye to the fantasy I held so tight: the relationship I wished for with my abuser. Today I will start thinking of a new picture and imagine ways I can be happy right now, with or without a relationship. Many abused women return to their abuser because they think the fantasy will come true, and they can't let go of that hope. Today I will not be one of them.

➤ *Day 62*

Do family members, including my children, keep reminding me of my past decisions? Are they hesitant to trust my ability to make wise choices now? Do they keep reminding me of my past mistakes? Do they ever say things to me that are hurtful? They may not mean to hurt me, but sometimes they do. I can let them know when their words or statements hurt my feelings. I might have to remind them, without going into detail, of all I'm doing to heal from my past and that I realize they care and worry about me. I may need to reassure them that I'm trying as hard as I can and learning as much as I can so that I won't end up in an abusive relationship again. Sometimes my loved ones need reassurance from me. Sometimes my children need to hear me say that the most important thing in my life is keeping them safe. Sometimes I need to remind myself that the most important thing in my life is keeping myself safe.

➤ Day 63

Today I understand that it's okay to ask for help. When I'm feeling overwhelmed, guilty, sad, depressed, unwanted, unloved, unworthy, or any other emotion that causes me to lose my perspective, I will ask for help from a trusted friend, support group, hot line worker, or therapist. I don't have to feel embarrassed or ashamed that I need someone to talk to, someone who can help me through difficult times. I can reach out to other people of my gender and welcome their opinions or advice. I can realize that although they might not fully understand how I feel, they can understand the dynamics of domestic violence and what it takes to heal from such an ordeal. I have the right to ask for support and understanding. I have the right to be heard. I have the right to do what it takes during my healing process to ensure that I move forward and not become stagnant. Recovery and healing are not about standing still; they're about taking each day as it comes, being willing to express myself honestly, and then being willing to listen.

➤ *Day 64*

Some days I might wish for affection, sex, or intimacy. This is perfectly normal, and I don't have to feel ashamed or embarrassed. Perhaps my last memories of my abuser—or what I choose to remember—are moments of intimacy. But wanting to be intimate with someone doesn't mean it has to be with my abuser, or with just anyone. If there's no one in my life with whom I feel safe enough to be intimate, I can choose not to have sex. I can use my energy in other areas instead. Today I will take exactly three minutes and make a list of things I can do instead of having sex. I will write as fast as I can, not stopping to analyze what I write. I will then look at my list and see how many things I wrote down that surprise me. Writing without stopping to think allows my mind to come up with options I might not normally consider. There are many alternatives to sex. Maybe I just want to be held or feel loved. But for now, if being close to someone who treats me with respect is not possible, I will try something different. I can use this technique anytime I want to come up with new ideas for creative outlets.

➤ *Day 65*

Today I will check in with myself. Have I been writing in my journal? Have I been working with a therapist or a support group? Have I been honest with myself? Have I been setting goals? Have I been totally committed to freedom from abuse? If any of these things are missing, I will try to understand why. Is something going on that I'm not willing to write about? Have I been caught up in old behavior? Am I too busy to keep up with my writing? Why haven't I been going to my group or therapist? Am I afraid of something? Have I taken a wrong turn somewhere? Is there something more I could be doing for myself? Am I in a relationship that isn't good for me? Today I will look at these reasons and get back on track. Today I will remind myself that my freedom from abuse must be the most important thing in my life, or it could cost me my life. Today I continue to want to live, to survive. I want to know what a life without abuse is, and I want that life to be mine.

➤ Day 66

While I was in an abusive relationship, I might have been forced to explain myself or my actions, and I might still feel that I have to do so. Today I will accept that I no longer have to explain my actions, especially to my children. If my children have taken on a protective or parental role with me, they might ask me why I make certain decisions or ask me to explain each detail of our lives. Today I will stop encouraging others, especially my children, to parent me in this way. I will let them know that it's my job to decide what's best for me and for us. Even though I'm aware that my past decisions may not have been wise, I can assure everyone that my way of thinking has changed. I might have confided in my children in the past, but today I will free them from this responsibility and allow them their place in the world as children. I might have to begin by simply telling them, "Because I'm the parent, and I said so," without further explanation. I can allow my family members their opinions and input, but I must also let them know that I will make the final decision. They might resist this, but knowing that I'm helping them to stop feeling responsible for me makes it easier.

Today I will take a moment to look at the meaning of domestic violence. It occurs when anyone we live with, used to live with, or are in a personal relationship with treats us in ways that are harmful. Domestic violence can affect us physically or hurt us emotionally. Emotional abuse can be just as damaging, if not more, and just as wrong as physical abuse. Today I'll be open to believing that people outside domestic situations can be abusive. Abuse can occur in the workplace, in schools, and in public settings. As I think about this, I'll also be aware that I don't want any form of abuse in any area of my life. I will begin thinking about all the people in my life and whether any of them might fit into the category of being abusive.

Today I will understand that almost all abusers have one thing in common: They can be quite charming when it suits them. Abusers can have different intellectual levels, different economic status, different backgrounds, different appearances, different values, different morals, different spiritual beliefs, different cultures, or different sexual orientations. The one thing that links them together is their ability to turn on the charm, win affection, and convince others that they're great people. Behind closed doors, however, they are different altogether. Once I got honest with others about my abuse, I might have gotten responses like "I thought he was such a nice guy" or "I just can't believe it, he's such a great father" or "I never would have guessed he could do that." If so, I can be reassured that whoever made those statements was just as taken in by my abuser's charm as I was. Knowing this helps me to be more cautious in the future. If I meet someone who seems to be kind, generous, and harmless, I will still watch for red flags, those intuitive warnings that help keep me safe.

Today I will continue to look at the people in my life who might be abusive to me or my family. To make it easier, I can rate them on a scale of one to five: one being seldom abusive and five being almost always abusive. As I rate these people, I will become more aware of the "fours" and "fives" in my life and what purpose they serve. Do I have to be around them? Do I have any options? Are they people from whom I should be protecting my children? Are they people with whom I could spend less time?

What would it take to get them out of my life? Do I need to make any changes in order to avoid these people? If so, what? If I feel that there are abusive people in my children's lives, I will do whatever it takes to protect them. I might need to have a meeting at their school or confront someone's parent. To protect myself, I might need to look for another job or make a formal complaint to my supervisor. By taking some kind of action, I can show my children and myself that being abused is not okay. I can prove to us all that I can do something about it.

If I'm looking for a new job, I will look not only for the job I want, but also for the manager or supervisor I want. When I go for an interview, I will pay attention to the person who will be my manager. Is this a person I can take instruction from? Does he care about his employees? Does she seem honest? Does he treat his employees fairly? Does she listen? Does he have good people skills? How does she relate to others in the company? Does he make degrading jokes about others? If the answers to these questions indicate that my potential supervisor is an abuser, I don't have to take the job. I have the right to decide whom I work for and that I won't accept abuse in the workplace. If my current supervisor is abusive, I don't need to quit today; I just need to plan for a change. Unless the abuse is serious, I can take the time I need to find a new job. I can discuss the situation confidentially with my direct supervisor or with upper management. I can also keep a journal of specific incidents at home, file a complaint, seek legal advice, or contact my union, human resources department, or labor commission. I deserve to be treated fairly and without abuse, in all areas of my life, even my workplace.

When I'm feeling abused in any situation, I can take the time to review the circumstances. In my past, I was the victim. Am I continuing to be the victim? Do I feel that others are out to get me, talking about me, being unfair to me, or don't like me? Am I caught up in past feelings of inadequacy? Do I feel that I'm an outsider? Are these things really happening, or am I creating them in my mind because of my past experiences? If I'm not sure, I can talk about my suspicions with my therapist, my support group, or a close friend. Most often, it helps to get someone else's viewpoint or opinion. I can share my thoughts of feeling mistreated or disliked with someone I trust. I'll also realize that I'm working on my self-esteem and learning how to appreciate my good qualities. The more I like myself, the less I will worry about what other people think of me.

➤ *Day 72*

When making decisions or viewing situations that involve others, I need to be aware of when I'm projecting my own feelings instead of considering those of others. Because my own feelings have been distorted or mixed up in the past, it might be hard to tell the difference between what others might actually be feeling and what I would be feeling if I were in their place. When looking at situations or making decisions that involve my children, I will be sure to ask them what they're feeling instead of assuming they have the same feelings that I do. I will encourage my children to be honest about their feelings and thoughts, and I'll help them know the difference between their own feelings and the feelings of others. When it comes to other people's feelings, instead of assuming they feel as I would, I will ask them how they feel and let them tell me. I will detach from my own feelings and allow other people in my life to have their own.

➤ *Day 73*

Today I will learn to be honest about my own thoughts and feelings instead of trying to please other people. In the past, I might have said anything to prevent my abuser from being angry with me or done anything to prevent a violent incident. I don't have to behave that way anymore. I have the right to my own thoughts, my own feelings, and my own behavior. I don't have to say or do things to control the situation. When I'm in situations with healthy people, I can speak my own mind and express myself in ways that are truthful to me. I can also teach my children how to express themselves honestly. We don't have to worry about "rocking the boat" or "walking on eggshells" anymore. We can say what we're thinking and tell the truth without fear of violence.

➤ *Day 74*

When I try new ways of expressing myself that feel more assertive, I might think that I'm supposed to feel better. But after I've set a boundary or talked about my feelings, I might not feel good about it. This is normal. People might ask me, "Now doesn't that feel good?" and my answer may be no. When I'm learning to stand up for myself and practice new ways of communicating, it might feel unfamiliar and even scary. I might feel that I'm being selfish or unkind. I might be afraid that people will leave me or not like me anymore. Today I will realize that I have the right to set my boundaries. I have the right to ask for what I need. I have the right to set limits in my life. I have the right to be my own person. Knowing this, I will continue to speak clearly about what I want and need, and eventually I will be able to express myself more easily.

Now that I know I have the right to express myself, I will learn how to do it in appropriate ways. I can say how I feel or ask for what I need without being mean or abusive to others. There's a very simple sentence I can use to express my feelings to others. I can say, "When you [their behavior], I feel [my feeling, not my thoughts], and what I need from you is [my need]." When I speak in this manner, people will know how I feel and what I need without my getting into unnecessary details or name-calling. It is easy, simple, clear, and honest. I can even choose to simply say, "What I need from you is [my need]." Using the word *I* in sentences such as "I need . . ." or "I feel . . ." helps me take responsibility for myself and move toward being an independent person. I'm glad to learn new ways of talking to other people that are healthy and thoughtful.

Has dishonesty played a part in my life? Have I felt the need to lie or stretch the truth in order to protect myself? Today I will notice when I'm being dishonest, and I'll ask myself why I feel the need to do so. Will I get hurt if I tell the truth? Will I lose something important if I tell the truth? Will someone be angry with me if I tell the truth? Will I be judged in a negative way if I tell the truth? I don't have to be dishonest in my life. I can tell the truth without fear of violence. If my actions are good for me and my children, I don't have to worry about what other people think of me. I can tell the truth and, beginning today, I will. I find comfort in knowing that the truth shall make me free. It might not happen all in one day, but by beginning to be honest right now, I'm freer than I ever was before when I thought I needed to lie.

➤ *Day 77*

There's a big difference between being dishonest and respecting my own privacy. There might be things that have happened in my past that I don't need or want to share with others. I don't have to share private thoughts or situations with everyone. I can choose when and with whom I will share this information. I can decide what I want to share with others without being dishonest. Telling the truth is necessary to move forward in my healing, but sharing every detail about myself is not. If people ask questions about my past and I don't feel comfortable answering them, I don't have to. I can simply say, "I don't feel comfortable discussing that" or "That's too personal, and I don't want to talk about it." When working with my therapist, I will be totally honest about everything. When I'm applying for a job or meeting new friends in a social setting, I can respect my own privacy by not revealing everything about me. I will use my best judgment when deciding what to share and when to be honest. Ultimately the most important person to be honest with is myself. Today I will be honest with myself and learn when to share personal information with others.

➤ *Day 78*

Sometimes it might be difficult to go to sleep. During these times I will practice imagery, which can relieve the pressures that prevent me from getting rest. I will lie down in a quiet place and close my eyes. I will envision a house that I've never seen before. I will imagine walking through the front door and looking around. What do I see? What color are the walls and furniture? What pictures are hanging on the walls? What plants or flowers are there? I imagine feeling totally at peace and totally safe. No one can harm me in this house. If I choose, I can imagine other people in the house. They all love me and want to support me. Perhaps they hug me or rock with me in a chair. They tell me how proud they are of me. I can stay in this house until I drift off to sleep. I'm always welcome here. When I need to rest, I can return to my imaginary house. I can change the surroundings, change the person or people in it, or be alone if I prefer. It can be anything I want it to be. It's a place where I can escape my worries or problems. It's a place where I feel safe and loved. It's a place I can rest.

➤ Day 79

Today feeling safe is easier. Many other women have been abused, and many are still being abused. I don't have to feel sorry for them. I can understand them. I know what it's like, and it's hard for me to think of them in their own situations. When I see news stories or articles about women being killed by their abusers, I can be sad for them, but it makes me so much more grateful to know that I don't have to live that life anymore. I got out. I broke free. I'm flying free in my new life. I'm making a difference in the statistics, making a difference in my own life, and making a difference in the lives of my family members and children.

➤ *Day 80*

Today I will practice patience. Do I become irritated when I don't get what I want and when I want it? Do I get frustrated in slow traffic? Do I yell at my family when I'm in a bad mood? Do I feel like screaming when I'm waiting in line at the store? When I'm feeling frustrated, moody, angry, or at the end of my rope, I will practice patience. I can take a deep breath and count to one hundred if I need to. I can write in my journal, take a walk, take a break, take a nap, or take a vacation. I can take a minute to look at my surroundings and get my priorities in order. Will the world really fall apart if I'm ten minutes late? What does anyone gain if I send my children to bed to the sound of my yelling? Will the line move any faster if I throw a fit? Probably not. I can tell myself that whatever is happening is just happening. I can either accept it or not. The choice is mine. I can't control my surroundings, but I can control my reactions to them.

➤ *Day 81*

Today I will forgive myself for ever thinking that any part of the abuse that I and perhaps my children endured was my fault. I didn't cause it, I couldn't cure it, and I dealt with it as best I could at the time. But back then, even my best became no longer good enough, and I left. I left to have a better life for myself and my children. I left because I couldn't take it anymore. I left because I knew there had to be something better. I left to save myself. I left because I was ready. But there are times when I still might hate myself for not leaving sooner. Today I will look in the mirror and say out loud, "I forgive you." I can say it as many times as I need to, through the pain, through the tears, through the disbelief. I will look into my own eyes and say, "I forgive you."

Today I will rest. I've been doing a lot of emotional work, and now it's time for a break. Do I cry easily? Am I quick to become angry? Have I been depressed? It's normal for my emotions to be close to the surface when I'm doing emotional work. I will allow myself my emotions. I can tell my children or loved ones that I may be feeling more sensitive or vulnerable lately. I can ask for their support and patience. I don't have to share my healing process with them if I choose not to. Today I will be gentle with myself, knowing that I'm exactly where I need to be—free.

Certain events or situations may trigger memories that are upsetting for me. A movie, the news, an article, or a certain sound might trigger a reaction that doesn't feel comfortable. I might not know why, only that it bothers me. I might even get a stomachache or a headache, feel sick, or become irritated or angry. I realize that many of my memories aren't pleasant, and I accept that about myself. I will remind myself that I'm making new memories. I will remind myself that whatever might be upsetting me is not necessarily about what's happening now; it has only reminded me of something that happened in the past. If my discomfort continues, I may choose to discuss it with my therapist. Perhaps a feeling is one that I need to look at more closely. Perhaps a memory needs to be addressed. I might need to work through an experience that has been too intense or traumatic to look at before now. I can seek professional help and support when troublesome feelings don't go away. I can remember that these triggers, or reminders, are not about my life today, but from a past that I'm leaving behind.

Thoughts or memories of my abuser might come to mind, and I might find myself feeling confused or consumed by them. I might be thinking about details of our relationship, whether they're painful or not. I might be overcome with mental images of him—or her—and not know how to make them stop. On these days, I can say out loud, "Leave me alone! I don't have to listen to you anymore!" Slowly but surely I'm letting go of these thoughts. Eventually, thoughts of my abuser will occur less often and for shorter periods of time. Dwelling on things that once were, or hoping they could have been different, doesn't help me today.

Fear of abandonment can most often be traced back to childhood. This fear began because, somewhere in the past, someone we loved either left us or wasn't there for us in the way we hoped he or she would be. Fear of abandonment might continue to affect our behavior and perception throughout our lives. Today I will accept that one of my fears is the fear of being abandoned. I will realize that this fear probably affected decisions I made for myself as well as decisions I made for my children. When I'm experiencing a fear of abandonment, I might ignore my boundaries. I might also ignore my own needs—or I might have in the past—to stop someone from leaving me. This fear can run so deep that I might not even be aware of its presence. I might find myself apologizing when I really don't mean it, or changing my mind when I don't really want to change it, and not understand why. Today I will think back to a time in my childhood when this fear might have begun. I will realize that I've probably carried this experience with me my whole life. I can choose to discuss this with my therapist or support group. I'm not alone in this fear, and I can talk about it in places that are safe.

➤ Day 86

Today I will be more aware of my fear of abandonment. I will notice when I'm afraid of someone leaving. When I find myself in this situation, I will consider the possibility of being alone. Would it be so bad if this person wasn't in my life? Would I be okay without him or her? Do I really need his or her friendship that much? Usually my childhood experience is affecting my current situation more than I know. When I can answer these questions honestly, I will be able to make decisions that are in my best interest. I don't have to make compromises in order to prevent someone from leaving. Once I become more aware of my fear of abandonment, I can recognize it, accept that it's about past experiences, set boundaries to protect who I am today, and move on.

➤ Day 87

Many violent relationships between couples include a dynamic, passionate sex life. The sex usually occurs during the honeymoon phase, when one or both people satisfy certain needs by having sex. The sexual experience is often extremely passionate and emotional, and many battered women confide that their best sexual experiences were those after a fight. The abuser may be trying to show remorse by pleasing his partner, and the abused woman may feel, temporarily, the intimacy and love she longs for. The sex is often so exhilarating because of the high energy level after the acute battering phase. Today I will remember the sexually exciting times I had with my abuser. Did I really want to have sex after he hurt me? Was I trying to please my abuser by having sex? Did I confuse sex with needing to be loved? I can become more aware of my perception of our sex life: how I viewed it then and how I can view it now. Were my needs really met? Did having sex make me feel better? Did it change anything? I will begin to look at my sexual experiences realistically, not romantically.

Today I will think about sexual abuse. Was I ever raped by my abuser? Was I ever forced or talked into having sex when I didn't want to? Did he make me do things I didn't want to do? Did he—or she—hurt me or threaten me during sexual activity? Did he force my children to watch? If so, today I will admit that I did not like being treated or hurt that way, and I did not agree to any of it. I might have thought about going to the police, but perhaps I didn't think they would believe me. My abuser might have threatened me or told me that no one would believe me. He might have told me that having sex with him was my duty. He might have told me that I deserved it. Some people who don't understand domestic violence would think that I liked it or I would have left. They don't understand me, and I don't have to question myself. The important thing is that I did not, and do not, like my body being abused in those ways. I did not deserve to be treated that way, it was not my fault, and it was not lovemaking. If I need support, I can contact a rape counselor or attend a sexual abuse survivor support group. Abusive sex is not love.

➤ Day 89

I will take the time I need to recover. There might have been experiences in my past from which I need to heal, and it might seem like such hard work. It *is* hard work, but I will take time to rest, recover, and heal. What happened to me was painful and left many scars, especially on the inside. I'm worthy of living through this, and I'm worthy of surviving. Who I am on the inside might not have been important to my abuser, but it is important to me. I like me and who I am.

➤ *Day 90*

Today I will do something that makes me laugh. I will watch a funny movie, have friends over to play table games, or act silly with my kids. I don't always have to be serious, and I have the right to enjoy my life. There might not have been very many things to laugh at in the past, but I want to have more fun now. I can have a pillow fight, tickle my kids, play dress-up, put on funny makeup, or tell funny stories. As long as I'm not hurting anyone, including myself, I will do today whatever makes me smile, giggle hysterically, or laugh out loud.

My abuser might have—and still might be—controlling me through money. I might have had to ask for money to buy what I needed. I might be dependent on him now for money to survive or care for the children. There are agencies that will help me get money for the children. I can call child support services and ask what I need to do to get help. If I don't have any children, I can look at my options for taking care of myself without his help. I can learn about handling money. I can ask a trusted friend or family member to help me make a budget, open a bank account, or learn to write checks. I can take a class or read books to learn more about handling my own finances. I might have to rent a room, get a roommate, or share a home temporarily. I don't have to be dependent on my abuser when it comes to money or financial matters. If for some reason I have no option but to be involved with him over money, I can consider finding a mediator or someone to help me communicate with him. Today I will begin to gain independence with my money.

Perhaps there were times when my abuser treated me like a servant or a waitress. I might have been expected to wait on him or his friends. There is a big difference between being a good host, entertaining, or taking care of my family and being treated like a servant. Today I will make a commitment that I will never be treated in that way again. I can decide for myself whom I want to care for. I do not have to serve, feed, do laundry, clean house, run errands, or provide any service for anyone against my will. I can make my own decisions when it comes to doing favors for my family, entertaining my guests, and doing household chores. Once I begin this process, I might find it difficult to create boundaries. Doing everything for everyone might have become a habit, but I can change it now by asking for help. Everyone in my household can contribute in some way, whether they help with the cooking or cleaning, or they simply pick up their own toys or dirty clothes. I will ask others to take responsibility for themselves. I will ask others to do their share.

If I've asked my children to help in the home but feel they aren't doing it, I might find myself feeling frustrated. I might feel like all I do is yell at them or constantly ask for their help, with little result. I might feel bad because I really don't want our lives to be like this. Today I will realize I have options. I can try different ways of encouraging them or teaching them responsibility. If my children are refusing to help, I can set up a program that consists of choices and consequences, or choices and rewards. We all need to learn that when we make certain choices, something happens. If we make wise choices, we should be rewarded. These rewards can be an allowance, special activities, prizes, or stickers on a chart. My children may have learned in the past that yelling and screaming are ways to get what we want, and they don't respond until they see that behavior. I need to teach my children about new ways of communicating, responsibility, and doing their share. We are all winners when we enjoy positive ways of working together.

Today I will take a look at jealousy. Was my abuser a jealous person? Was I wrongfully accused of things I didn't do? Was I prevented from dressing the way I wanted to dress because it might make him jealous? Was I forced to stay home or isolated because of his jealousy? Were there ever violent incidents or fights because of his jealousy? Today I will make a list of the things my abuser wouldn't let me do or accused me of doing because of his jealousy. When I'm finished, I will read the list and remember how I felt when I had to follow his rules or was blamed for something I didn't do. Jealousy usually occurs when someone has low self-esteem. Jealous people become suspicious of others and, because of their own sense of inadequacy, feel that they're being betrayed. Today I will admit that there's no room in my life for jealousy, and I will not accept it anymore. I can choose my own clothes, choose where I go, choose my own friends, choose my own hobbies, and choose my own goals. As long as I'm keeping myself safe, I can make my own decisions without fear of someone else being jealous. Someone else's suspicions or accusations don't affect me anymore.

➤ *Day 95*

Am I a jealous person? Did I distrust my abuser? Did my abuser have affairs or openly flirt with others? Today I will make a list of the times I felt jealous. When I'm finished, I will read the list and remember how it felt to feel jealous or betrayed. Whether or not I had a reason to be jealous in the past, today I will let it go. I will remember that most of the time I felt jealous, it was because I didn't believe I was worth being loved. I also might not have believed my abuser could be faithful, so I assumed he wouldn't be. If my abuser did betray my trust, he might have tried to blame it on me by saying that I drove him to it. He might have told me that if I acted or looked different, he wouldn't have had to do it. Today I will realize that I did not cause my abuser to be unfaithful or lie. I will realize it wasn't my fault and that I deserve a relationship with someone who can be honest and loyal. When I enter into new relationships, I will notice if I'm feeling jealous. I will determine whether it's caused by feelings of low self-esteem or whether someone truly isn't being honest with me. Trust is difficult, given my past, but I'm willing to be in a relationship in which I can trust and be trusted.

➤ *Day 96*

Today I will begin telling the truth. If I've found myself being dishonest in the past, and for no apparent reason, I will stop today. I will also recall the times when I was a child that I felt afraid to be honest and lied because I felt I needed to protect myself. I will make a list of all the times in my childhood when this happened. This is the start of learning how to be honest with myself. I don't have to show my list to anyone, just be mindful of it.

Today I will look at my list from yesterday. Is it finished? Do I have more to add to it? When my list is complete, I will write next to each experience what I most feared would happen if I told the truth. When I'm finished, I will review my list. Is there a pattern? Do certain reasons for lying appear on the list more than once? What was the thing I feared most? Did my fears come true? Did I get caught in my lies? If I didn't get caught, what were the rewards? What did I get out of the lies? Was it better for me to lie? Was there something that didn't happen because I lied? Remembering my feelings as a child gives me insight into whom I've grown up to be. I can forgive myself for telling lies as a child. I can forgive myself for being afraid. I can understand that I did the best I could at that time. I can understand myself and love myself. Today I will accept the fact that there were times, as a child, when I was afraid. I can accept the fact that I lied for my own reasons. Lying was a way I thought I could keep myself safe.

➤ *Day 98*

Today I will take it easy. I will accept that I've made mistakes in the past. I will also accept that I did the best I could. Maybe I wish I had made different decisions or handled things differently. But wishes don't change the past. I can only begin making changes today. I will accept myself, knowing that I did my best. I did what I thought I had to do. I am and have always been worthy of being loved the way I want to be loved.

Today I will make a list of the times I lied to my abuser. Next to each experience, I will write what I feared would happen if I told the truth. When I'm finished, I will review my list. Is there a pattern? Do certain reasons for lying appear on the list more than once? What were the things I feared most? Did my fears come true? Did I get caught in my lies? If I didn't get caught, what were the rewards? What did I get out of the lies? Was it better for me to lie? Was there something that didn't happen because I lied? Remembering my fears while being abused gives me insight into why I might have stayed. Today I will accept that I was afraid. I can forgive myself for lying because I was afraid. I understand that I did the best I could at the time. Today I will accept the fact that there were times when I lied to my abuser to protect myself. Lying was a way to keep myself safe.

➤ *Day 100*

I'm right where I'm supposed to be. I'm proving to myself that I'm strong and courageous, simply because I'm willing to be where I am in my healing. I will have an open mind, listen to others, and make informed decisions. Even when I become afraid, I will feel the fear and accomplish my goals anyway. I will be aware of how my fear feels inside my body. Does my heart beat faster? Do I hold my breath? Do I feel nauseous? Do I have a burst of energy? Do I want to crawl under the covers and hide? I'm willing to feel my fear without having to do anything to change it. I will allow myself to feel whatever it is I'm feeling. I've had many experiences that made me afraid. Today is different, because I don't have to make the fear go away. I'm allowing myself to be right where I am and experience all my emotions honestly.

➤ Day 101

Today I will make a list of the lies I told about my abuse. What did I tell people when I was bruised or battered? What did I say when I couldn't go somewhere with friends? What did I tell people when my abuser yelled at or criticized me? What did I say so other people wouldn't know what I was going through? Whom was I protecting? Was it my abuser, or was it myself? Did I not want other people to know what was happening to me? Was I ashamed? Did I not want to create any more problems? What was I afraid of? What did I think would happen if others knew the truth? I can write about these fears and talk about them to someone with whom I feel safe. Remembering I lied because I was afraid helps me forgive myself today. Whatever my reasons were for lying, I don't have to do it anymore. I can choose to share the truth with people I trust or not to talk about it at all. Respecting my own privacy is not being dishonest; it's having the courage to decide what's best for me.

➤ *Day 102*

Today I will forgive myself for being dishonest about my abuse. I realize that I was afraid and did the best I could under the circumstances. I didn't mean to lie to my friends or family; I was doing what I thought I had to do. I didn't mean to hurt anyone, and I let go of any guilt I have over it. If I choose to do so, I can apologize to my family members. But I can also explain that I did what I thought I needed to do at the time. I can ask for their support in my journey of healing and ask them to understand that I didn't mean to hurt them. I can tell my loved ones that I was in so much pain, I couldn't see or think of anyone else's pain. I will understand that it was okay for me to protect myself. Being dishonest was a survival skill that I learned how to use. It served me then, but I no longer need it.

I've now had time to learn that I don't have to explain myself, especially to my children. I'm allowing them their childhood without encouraging them to feel responsible for me. I'm leaving them out of my process but telling them of my decisions. Depending on their ages, I can now decide which situations deserve an explanation. I might want to explain why I want to live in a certain neighborhood or why I want to take a certain job. I might explain why they need to help clean up or why they need to go to bed at a certain time. I can begin to explain to my children, or others, some of my actions and decisions. I can acknowledge that I've gone from telling them almost everything to telling them nothing. Now it's time to find a middle ground. I can now begin to explain myself in some matters, but I will decide what those are. If my children have a need to be included in decisions, I will point out the decisions they're able to make for themselves. They might decide what they wear or eat, when they brush their teeth, what classes they take, or what TV shows they see. There are decisions that they can make, but as their parent, I will make the final decisions on important issues in our lives.

➤ *Day 104*

Today I will review the goals I've set for myself. Are they still realistic? Are they still goals I want to attain? Are they closer in reach now? Have I forgotten them or become discouraged in working toward them? I might need to make new goals or begin working harder toward my current goals. I can achieve my goals if I'm committed to them, because goals don't just happen. I will never achieve my goals unless I'm making the effort. Today I will begin or continue to work toward the goals that are most important to me. I will also change the ones that aren't as important as they used to be.

Today I will learn how to be more in touch with the intensity of my feelings. I will practice rating my feelings on a scale of one to ten: one being almost nonexistent and ten being extremely intense. I can share and practice this technique with my family and my children. When we are talking about how we feel, one of us can say, "I feel angry," and the others can ask, "What number is it?" Once we rate the intensity of our feeling by using a number, we all have a clearer picture of the feeling. I can also use this scale to get a better idea of my own feelings. After a few minutes of experiencing a feeling, I might ask myself how I would rate it. This way, I can determine whether it's lessening or becoming stronger. This technique can help me become more aware of how my feelings change, stay the same, or go away. It also helps me communicate better, instead of ignoring how I feel or acting in ways that confuse others.

Have I ever made a list of people in my life who have abused me? Today I will make that list or complete it if I've already started it. When I'm finished, I will put the names on it in order, starting with my first abuser and ending with my most recent. I'll continue this exercise by describing how each person hurt me, then by adding any early warning signs I noticed prior to the abuse. What happened before the relationship became abusive? Did this person try to control me from the beginning? Early on in the relationship, did this person act in ways that didn't feel quite right? Was this person abusive from the beginning? How did the abuse start? This list may take longer than a day to complete, but I will take all the time I need. I may choose to share it with my therapist or counselor, or I may want to keep it to myself. My list should provide a clearer picture of all my experiences in abusive relationships. Being aware of my relationship history helps me to make better choices in future relationships. I will now be able to see similar warning signs in new relationships and make more informed choices about new friends.

Today I will look at my list from yesterday and write about how I felt during these abusive relationships. Do I notice a pattern in my feelings about the abuse? Did I feel isolated? Did I feel alone? Did I feel unloved? Did I feel unworthy? Did I feel numb? Did I feel trapped? I will write about all the feelings I had during the abuse in my life. I can be gentle with myself and realize I don't have to complete this list today. I can love myself, be easy on myself, and understand that it took years to live this list. Therefore, I can take all the time I need to write it.

Today I will complete my abuser list. After I'm finished, I will write next to each name the things I would like to say to that particular abuser. It doesn't matter whether the person is out of my life, still has contact with me, or is deceased. I will write the statements I would say to each one of the people who has abused me. There may be one thing, many things, or pages of things I'd like to say. I can say anything, as many times as I need to. I can write for as many hours or days as I need to. I can even add to the list in the days to come. I can experience the anger, the pain, the betrayal, the sadness, or whatever emotion I might have. Through it all, I'll be totally convinced that I'm ready to live without being hurt, battered, humiliated, abused, tormented, belittled, or ignored. I can say to myself, "Despite everything that all of you have done to me, I'm here, I matter, I'm important, and I will be heard."

➤ Day 109

Every single day brings new experience, awareness, and knowledge. I can find something each day that is proof of my accomplishments. It might be that I'm now ready to live without pain or violence. I might notice, upon waking, that I'm not afraid of what might happen in my own home. I don't need to worry that I might say the wrong thing or make a mistake, according to someone else. I will know that each new day brings the opportunity to be glad that no one is hitting or belittling me. My worries today are different, my fears today are different, and I'm different too, thanks to me.

There might be days when I don't feel proud or successful. There might be times when I'm critical of myself or how my life is going. It's okay to feel sad or depressed. All my emotions are part of me, and I can accept them for being just that. If there are changes that need to be made, I can choose to make those changes. If I'm just feeling a little down, I don't have to force myself to feel happy. I can be right where I am, for today. I can allow myself the room and time to be normal. Normal people experience all their emotions, and they don't have to change them for someone else.

➤ *Day 111*

Today I will think of the things I like about myself. Am I smart? Am I creative? Am I a good mother? Am I good friend? Am I a good employee? Am I a good cook? Am I a good gardener? Am I a good writer? What are the good qualities that I possess? Am I honest? Am I a good listener? Do I express myself well? If I were choosing me as a friend, what are the things I would most like about me? It's important to take time to evaluate myself and look at my strong points. If I don't see them, perhaps it's difficult for me to believe that other people could see them. We all have our shortcomings, but what are the good things about me? Today I will think about what I like about myself.

➤ *Day 112*

Today I will catch up on the things I need to complete. I will take notice of the things I've started, and I'll work toward their completion. If I'm current with things I need to do, I can use this time to rest and do nothing. Have I been procrastinating? Have I been putting something off until later that I can do now? I will look at my list of responsibilities or suggested activities, and today I will begin—or complete—those things I said I would do later. Today is about completion.

➤ *Day 113*

Are there things I need to say that I haven't said? Is there someone I need to call? Have I thought about a person in my life on more than one occasion and didn't tell him or her? Besides my abuser, who in my life do I have a relationship with that is not current or up-to-date? We never know what tomorrow will bring, and we don't know whether the people who matter most will always be there. Today I will make a genuine effort to tell the important people in my life how I feel about them. When speaking to people I love, I will never leave their company on an angry or sour note. If I thought this was the last time I would ever talk to them, what would I say? Today is about further completion, closure, and keeping my relationships up-to-date.

If I'm looking for a new or different job, I will pay attention to the person I will be working for, as well as what my job responsibilities will be. While it might be a good job, I must realize that my supervisor, manager, or employer will have a huge influence on my work environment as well. If I enjoy my work but have an abusive boss, I will be caught once again in another form of an abusive relationship, and this is not for me. A job interview is also my opportunity to interview a prospective employer. I can ask questions about workplace policies, job responsibilities, open-door policies (which allow me to go to someone in a higher position if I don't find a solution with my immediate supervisor), or anything else that might be important for me to know. I can take responsibility for my safety in a new workplace.

➤ Day 115

Before I consider taking a new job, I will request that everything I've discussed or negotiated with my potential employer be put in writing. This is not uncommon, and it prevents my potential employer from changing his or her mind or backing out of agreements; it also protects me in case a different decision-maker tries to change the employment conditions under which I was hired. An employer who is not willing to provide this is probably not someone for whom I want to work. Without these agreements or conditions in writing, employers can change the job require-ments or responsibilities, and there's nothing that can be done about it. My request also keeps me in a position of having clarity in my life and asks a certain respect from others. In the past, parts of my life were not defined or clear. Things were usually "up in the air" and confusing. Today I want things to be out in the open, without any guesswork. I will ask for clarity before making employment decisions.

➤ Day 116

If I'm not treated in a respectful or appropriate manner, I will write about these situations. I will not be abused or treated badly. If I'm not already keeping a journal, I will begin now. Keeping a journal helps me better know what is okay with me and what is not. I can keep my journal in a private, safe place, and I don't have to show it to others. I will also notice when I'm creating problems. Am I gossiping? Am I starting trouble? Am I bored? Am I creating a crisis where there wasn't one? Am I acting in an abusive way? I will take responsibility for my own actions wherever I am. When an abusive situation is serious, I can learn about the laws in my state by contacting an attorney or going to the library. If an abusive situation has not broken the law, I can write about it for myself. If it continues to bother me, I can speak to my therapist about it. I have the right to keep track of problems or abusive situations. I have the right to take legal action when a law has been broken.

Today I will continue to protect my children. Are my children having problems at school? Are their grades slipping, or are they obsessed with getting good grades? Are they complaining about their school, classes, or teachers? Do they understand their homework? Do they feel good about themselves in school? If I have concerns, I can make an appointment with their teachers, guidance counselor, principal, or other appropriate professionals. Because there are so many students in classrooms, when my children have special needs, the only one who can make a difference might be me. I might need to explain to someone that my children are healing from domestic violence. I might need to stand up for my children and ask for help. Today I will be more aware about my children's needs in school, and I will do something about them. I will prove to my children, and myself, that I can be there for them when they need me. They might be angry with me, thinking I wasn't there for them in the past. But today, I will show them that they can depend on me.

If I have young children in day care, I will pay close attention to their attitudes and feelings about their caregiver or day-care environment. Are my children happy? Are they being picked on? Are they bullying or hurting other children? I might need to explain to my day-care provider or other parents that my children are healing from domestic violence. I might need to stand up for my children and ask for help. I might need professional help in handling these problems, or I might have to find another day-care facility or provider. Today I will take care of and protect my children by being aware of their educational and emotional needs. Today I will take care of and protect myself by being aware of my own emotional needs. I will look for and ask for help when necessary.

At some point, I might meet someone I find physically attractive or who has characteristics I'm drawn to. It might stir up past feelings of desire. While I can acknowledge these feelings, I don't have to act on them. If I feel an instant connection with this person, there's a chance I might be repeating old relationship patterns that aren't good for me. I need to break these patterns by choosing better relationships. I can do so by being aware of what attracted me to my abuser. Am I attracted to someone who seems exciting or dangerous, who enjoys living on the edge or appears to be physically or emotionally strong? Do I mistake jealousy for caring? What draws me to certain types of people? I can now choose relationships with people who have strength of character, moral strengths, or the strength of knowing how to be kind and loving. I can avoid relationships where there's a hasty attraction. At this point in my life, love at first sight does not exist. The best thing I can do for myself is to take the time to get to know someone to whom I'm attracted. I can set boundaries and pay attention to how this person reacts to everyday life. I'm not willing to repeat past relationship mistakes.

➤ *Day 120*

Am I still keeping gifts my abuser gave me? Do I have dried flowers or photos in a scrapbook, lingerie, or mementos of our intimate relationship? Can I think of a good reason why I should save them? Are there things in my home that we bought together or things that he especially liked? Can I think of a good reason to save them too? Chances are, I can't. Instead, I can choose to give them away or throw them away. Do I have other mementos, such as the bandages I wore after he battered me? Did I save the pieces of things that he broke? Did I keep tearstained tissues? I don't need to save reminders of the violence any more than I need to save intimate or meaningful reminders of my abuser. Today I will continue to clean out my life. Moving forward also means letting go of what I don't need, and I don't need to be reminded of intimate or violent moments with my abuser.

Today I will review the goals I've set for myself. Have I met some of them? Do some of them seem out of reach? If so, I will consider how I can simplify them by breaking them down into smaller goals. If one of my goals is to live in a nicer house, I'll look at ways I can begin to work toward that goal. Do I already know what kind of house I want? Where is it? What does it look like? How much will it cost? Perhaps I can change my spending habits, save more money, or begin to establish my credit. I might simply picture my new house in my mind or cut out a picture and tape in on my mirror. If one of my goals is to have a specific career, I will get a catalog from a college and find out what classes might prepare me for that career. Perhaps I could go to a career training school, work toward a promotion at my current job, or get my GED. I can ask for the help I need to accomplish this. Today I will choose one goal that seems hard to reach and make a list of the steps necessary to achieve it. When I work toward my goals one step at a time, I can feel successful with each day.

Do I have a collage or scrapbook that I've made in the past? Are the pictures or phrases in it still accurate representations of what I want in my life? Is there something I want to add or change? Do I want to create a different or new picture? I can find new pictures to add to my collection or make something entirely new. I will encourage my children to do the same for themselves. We can do this activity together, or I can support them in finding the materials they need to make their own collage or scrapbook. This activity can create healthy and open communication between us as a family. I will not tell them what they should want, nor will I question their ideas. I will allow them to choose pictures of their own and create their own collections in their own way. I can love and support my children in their individuality and encourage them to think about what they want in their lives.

How do I react to the problems in my life? When something doesn't happen or someone doesn't behave the way I would like, how do I act? Do I scream or throw things? Do I withdraw and refuse to talk about it? Do I tell my story to anyone who will listen, repeating it over and over? Today I will focus on solving my problems and dealing with them effectively. I can choose to react in appropriate ways, without being abusive, violent, or overly dramatic. Part of my healing from abuse is learning how to live without crisis and drama. Am I making a big deal out of something that's insignificant? Am I looking for others to sympathize with me and perhaps feel sorry for me? What am I looking for when I act in ways that aren't good for me? I can learn how to deal with problems in ways that make sense. I can write about them, talk about them to my group or counselor, look at my options for solving them, and then try to resolve them. If I'm upset about a situation over which I have no control, I will simply accept that I have no control. There will be problems in my life that I can't solve, and I will accept that. I don't have to like it, but I will accept it.

➤ *Day 124*

I don't always get to know why. I may find myself caught up in wondering why something happened while asking myself, "What did I do wrong?" or "Why did this happen to me?" If the situation is something I can change, I can plan how to change it. I can look at my options or ask someone else's opinion and ultimately decide what to do. If the situation is one in which I have no control, I might never get to know why it happened. I might have to understand that it just did. When I'm wondering why, sometimes the hardest answer to accept is that there isn't one. I won't always understand or be given the reasons for certain situations. I will do my best to accept that sometimes things are the way they are.

➤ Day 125

Today I will practice staying in the moment. Staying in the moment doesn't mean I can't plan for my future, set goals, or be optimistic. Staying in the moment means that I don't let my mind wander to past experiences, get caught up in fantasies, or become consumed with false hopes. I will learn how to focus on each moment as it happens. Is there something going on in my life that I need to attend to? Is there someone who needs my attention? Have I been ignoring the present because I'm thinking too much about things that have happened or that might happen in the future? Recovering from the past and making plans for the future are necessary tasks, but I also need to pay attention to the way things are right now.

➤ *Day 126*

When people refuse to talk to their loved ones about important feelings, it is a form of abuse. When we shut out the people with whom we have close or intimate relationships, we are not participating in those relationships to their fullest. By not talking, I'm leaving other people to guess how I'm feeling. They might not understand me because I haven't given them any information. I might then resent them for misunderstanding me or not giving me what I need. In order to be understood or to have my needs met, I need to talk about them with others. Perhaps, in the past, I learned that talking about my feelings only led to problems. Perhaps I was criticized for feeling the way I did. Maybe others didn't listen or didn't hear me the way I needed to be heard. I might have felt that if I did share my feelings, I would be rejected or hurt. Being open about myself still might be a very scary thought, but today I will practice expressing my feelings to the people who care about me. It's only fair to them, and to me.

➤ Day 127

The abuse that I experienced in the past was frightening. I might have become so used to scary incidents or experiences that I lost my perspective of what is scary and what is not. I might have become overly sensitive to sounds, little things I notice, or comments people make. I might find myself feeling afraid when there seems to be no reason. I can learn to listen to my intuition when it comes to my safety. Do I feel uncomfortable walking to my car in the dark? Do I check, more than once, to see if I've locked all the doors at night? Do I sleep with a light on? Do I cross the street when I see an oncoming stranger who looks unusual? When I'm in situations where I feel afraid and feel the need to protect myself, it's okay for me to do so. Even though I'm recovering from a past filled with fear, I don't have to ignore the feeling I get when I'm frightened. Even though I might have been told repeatedly that it was all in my mind, or that I was making a big deal out of nothing, I can take the necessary steps to keep myself safe when I'm afraid.

➤ *Day 128*

Just as I will take the steps necessary to protect myself, I will also be aware of when I might be ignoring possible danger. While I might have become overly sensitive in some respects, I might not be sensitive enough in others. Do I leave my keys in my car at the store? Do I not lock my doors? Do I walk on dark streets without thinking of my safety? Do I consider the safety of my children at all times? Do I take the necessary steps to protect myself and my children, or have I become numb or aloof when it comes to danger? I will begin to pay attention to my surroundings and be realistic about possible dangerous situations. I might even have to force myself to imagine what could happen in order to decide. Without being overly protective or paranoid, I can find a balance between being careful and being careless.

Do I find myself shying away from meeting new people because I'm afraid of what might happen? Am I reluctant to go to parties or social gatherings because I might meet someone like my abuser and that person will hurt me? Do I refrain from going out with people from work because I don't trust them? Today I will understand that having good friends is important to my recovery. Although it's equally important not to trust too much too soon, I can begin to take the hand of those who might be reaching out to me. I can keep my privacy and make new friends at the same time. I can have friends but not become too dependent on them. I can learn how to have casual friendships without being preoccupied with the fear that these friends will abandon me. Once I begin to feel my own sense of worth and realize that I'm a likable person who is fun to be with, provides good company, and has much to offer, I'll be able to believe that others will think so too. If I refuse to make friends because of what might happen or out of fear that I'll get hurt, I will probably spend a lot of time alone. I'm ready to enjoy my life instead of living in fear.

Do I still find myself wanting to know about my abuser? Do I ask questions or call others to find out about him? Do I still allow him to call me? Do I find myself wondering what he's doing now or where he is? Am I curious about what's happening in his life? Today, and any other day, I will not spend any time thinking about my abuser or his situation. I don't have to use any part of my new life wondering about what he's doing in his. It doesn't matter if he has a new relationship or has moved on. The only information I need to have is that which affects my safety or the safety of my children. I will not engage in conversation about him, things that are happening to him, his plans, his troubles, or anything that involves him. If there's information I should have, I can ask an attorney, a close friend, or a women's advocate to contact me in those cases. I don't need to speak to my abuser when he wants to speak to me. I'm not his best friend, counselor, sponsor, therapist, or confidant. I'm done worrying or caring about his life, and what he does is no longer of importance to me.

When other people are abusive to me, I don't have to make excuses for them. They might have confided that they've had a troubled past or are going through a rough time. They might have told me how unfair their life is, and they might claim that no one likes or appreciates them. I don't have to be the person who fixes their lives. I don't have to take on the role of making them feel better. When other people are abusive to me, there is no excuse. I deserve to be treated with kindness and to experience friendships in which there is give-and-take. I deserve to get the love that I give back in return. There is no excuse for anyone to treat me badly, including my past abusers.

When the people in my life share their problems or challenges with me, I can detach enough to be a good listener. If I believe they're making mistakes, I can express my opinion by saying, "In my experience . . ." or "From what I've seen . . ." or "I believe. . ." I can take responsibility for my own opinions and offer advice without telling others what they should do. We all have the right to make our own decisions. Just as I appreciate when I've been allowed my own decisions, I can respect that others need to make their own decisions too. Even if I believe that I can see their situations more clearly than they can, I can detach enough to allow them their own mistakes. I can be a good friend by being there for them when they need me and, at the same time, not allow them to use me when they make the same mistakes over and over. I can offer my advice without telling other people what to do.

➤ Day 133

There might be times in my current relationships when I feel like I'm the only one who cares. If I'm being a good friend, am I getting anything in return? Am I always the one who initiates the phone calls? Am I the one making all the invitations to dinner? Am I always the one listening, without having any chance to talk about myself? I deserve to have friendships and relationships in which I get something in return. I deserve to feel appreciated and needed, but I also deserve to appreciate and need others. Today I will evaluate my relationships to see if I'm happy in them. I deserve to have my needs met and not be limited to meeting the needs of others.

Amends are acts of communication in which we try to correct something in a past or current relationship. We might be trying to "fix" the relationship and get it back on track, or we might simply be trying to take responsibility for something we did wrong. Amends can be taken as an apology or as a way of acknowledging our part in a problem and showing regret. Is there anyone in my past or present with whom I need to make amends? Is there something that has gone unsaid that I now need to say? Have I hurt someone without meaning to? Were my actions harmful to someone else, but I wasn't aware of it until now? Today I will make a list of the people with whom I need to make amends. I can think about each person as I write his or her name, making a note about what I might say. I will keep in mind that amends are for me. I might not get the forgiveness I hope for, and the person I've hurt—or I—might not want to keep or resume our friendship. Amends are a way I—and I alone—can experience closure and personal growth.

If I have unrealistic expectations when making my amends, I won't be able to feel a sense of accomplishment by doing so. As part of leaving my past behind, I will make an attempt to bring closure to unresolved relationships. I don't have to make amends to my abuser in person. If there is anything that needs to be said, I can do it by writing for myself alone. I can also do this in the cases of people who are deceased or whose whereabouts are unknown to me. I will set a target date by which my amends need to be completed, and I'll keep that agreement with myself. Amends are for my own healing, and I will begin them today.

I do not have to make spur-of-the-moment decisions. I can take a reasonable amount of time to think about my options, look at the potential results, and make informed, careful decisions. If I find that I have a problem making decisions for myself, I will practice by making small decisions first. When I practice making smaller decisions, I'll become more in tune with what I want. This will make the more difficult decisions easier. I need to know what I want before I can decide things for myself. But I will also be aware that I don't have to hurry; I can take my time.

If I haven't been doing so lately, today I will look at my worry wall. Are there things that need to be moved or taken down? Are there new worries in my life that I need to put on the wall? When I put new worries on the wall, do I place them as high as I used to? How much am I worrying as compared with before? Perhaps I'm learning that worrying doesn't really change the outcome of a situation. Worrying is a waste of my energy, and I can use this energy to accomplish more positive tasks.

Do I find that I have extra time on my hands? Do I find that I'm bored or have nothing to do? I can find out what volunteer programs are available in my community. Giving my time and energy to others is a kind of exchange for all the help I've been given. When others were there for me, I appreciated it and learned from it. Now it's my turn to give something back. Maybe I can donate an hour or two a day, or a couple of days a week, to an organization or charity in my community that needs my help. If I don't have extra time, perhaps I can go through my old clothes and donate them to a shelter. I can also make a donation to a charity or club. Today I will learn how it feels to willingly give something back in exchange for what I've received.

Do I ever find myself around people who are negative? Are these people constantly complaining or criticizing others or their situation? Am I starting to feel like they're affecting my attitude or outlook? I don't have to give other people that much power over my life. I can choose how I feel and what kind of attitude I have. I don't have to listen to the negativity of others. I can set an example for them by making positive statements or by having a positive attitude toward them. Some people simply aren't happy unless they're unhappy. Today I will choose not to be one of them. I have many things in my life to be grateful for, and I will not let the negativity of others affect me.

➤ *Day 140*

If I think that I can live my life without being exposed to any form of violence, I might be wrong. There is violence all around me: on TV, in the newspaper, on the radio, or even in the life of someone I know. I can learn how to deal with my anger and teach my children how to deal with theirs to ensure that we feel safe in our house. Doing this doesn't necessarily mean that we will never experience violence in our lives again. While I don't have to like this, I can accept that violence is part of life. Today, however, I will know that I don't have to live with it in my house.

➤ *Day 141*

Do I find that I'm constantly late or rushing in the morning? Do I feel like I'm racing around trying to get somewhere on time? Do I yell at my kids to hurry, and is the last memory they have of me as they go about their day one of me screaming? Today I will plan my time more effectively. I can set the alarm earlier, go to bed sooner, or change my schedule in some way to give myself more time. Is my reason for hurrying really so important that I can't send my children off with a hug or a positive word? Today I will change the way I begin my day to one with better timing and more loving communication. I can give myself and my family the gift of having enough time for them.

➤ *Day 142*

Are there people in my life whom I need to thank?
Is there someone whom I need to call or write and
thank for all he or she has done for me? Today I will
practice keeping current with others by thanking
the people who deserve to know I appreciate them.
Perhaps there was a counselor, women's advocate,
nurse, or volunteer who seemed especially nice or
who went out of his or her way for me. I can thank
these people by calling them or sending a card or
letter. In order to appreciate how far I've come, I
need to thank those who helped me get here.

➤ *Day 143*

Today I will let go of always having to know why. I don't have to analyze or explore the meaning of everything that has happened to me. I don't have to wonder if I was being punished or did something to deserve such abusive treatment. I don't have to figure out what it all means. I can let go of having to know why and be satisfied with knowing it just is. Just as I might answer a child who asks why the sky is blue or why water is wet, I can tell myself, "It just is."

➤ *Day 144*

I don't always have to like how I feel. There might be days when I don't feel energetic or feel like working toward a goal. There might be days when I'm in a bad mood or just want to be left alone. It is okay for me to have these kinds of days and these kinds of feelings. I can accept that I don't always have to be positive and happy. My life isn't always going to feel great, and today I will accept that I don't always have to like it. Negative feelings and moods are temporary and will fade as quickly as they appeared.

Today I will plan to have quality time with my children. When I feel that I'm too often telling my children, "I'm busy" or "wait until later," I can plan a certain time when we can talk or do an activity of their choice. During this time I will not answer the phone, watch TV, work, or do anything but be with my children. It doesn't take very much time to satisfy a child. Our special time can be half an hour or even fifteen minutes a day. If my children are old enough, I may even choose to take a day off and have a special day with them. Part of having balance in my life is spending some special time with my children, time that is scheduled and planned. I need to spend time with them and be consistent in doing so. Being consistent helps me develop trust in my children by showing them that I mean what I say and that they can depend on me.

I can't control the way other people feel about me or what they think about me. I don't have to live my life or make decisions based on trying to please others. If others don't believe in me, trust me, or like what I'm doing, I can allow them their own opinion, but I don't have to give them any power in my life. I can be proud of myself and let that be enough. I can know that I'm trying as hard as I can, and I'm progressing at my own pace. If the opinions of other people are not justified, I don't have to let them bother me. I can't make people feel a certain way or have a particular belief. The only person I have control over is me.

➤ Day 147

Many people feel that women should play a certain role. They might believe that women should be the caretakers, the cooks, the housekeepers, and the ones who keep the family together no matter what. I don't have to live my life based on traditional roles. I can be my own person, making plans according to what I want in my own life. Tradition may have its place in certain areas of my life, but I don't have to give up who I am to fit a particular role. I can take notice of who I am and who I want to be, and I can live my life the way I choose. I don't have to fit into the stereotype that others may have of me. I'm strong enough to decide what I want in my life and go after it.

➤ *Day 148*

When I meet someone whom I'm interested in dating, I will take it slowly. I will take the time to get to know this person, and I'll be careful not to share too much, too soon. I will remember my past relationship patterns. Did my relationships move too fast? Did my partners buy me gifts when they didn't know me very well? Did they make plans for the two of us that seemed too intimate? Did they expect too much, too soon? Did they presume to know me before really getting to know me? When meeting new people, I don't have to hurry. I can take all the time I need to get to know them. Perhaps I'll feel safest meeting them in public places for a while. I don't have to introduce them to my children until I feel they're trustworthy. I don't have to invite them to my home before I'm ready. I deserve to feel safe, and I will take precautions that ensure my safety. I can take things as slowly as I need to in new relationships.

If I've entered into a relationship that I feel might become intimate, I will be a good listener for my children. Perhaps they have their own reservations, their own fears, and their own anger to deal with. They may not want me to date or become involved again. They may fear for my safety or their own. I will listen to their feelings and encourage their expression. I will support their feelings, respect them, and discuss them. I will remind my children that this relationship is not with our past abuser, and I'll ask for their trust in my decisions. I will tell them that they're my highest priority and make sure that they are. I will tell them that I will not make any decisions or choices that would endanger them or myself. I will go slow enough in this relationship that they will have time to adjust and trust. I will not force them to accept anyone in their lives when they're not ready. I will not force them to like someone before they're ready. I will allow them to move at their own pace. If I've made a good decision about whom I'm dating, my children will see this over time and feel more at ease. I can take the time I need for myself and allow my loved ones the time they need too.

Arguing is very different from fighting. When two people are fighting, one of them is trying to win. In a healthy argument, there doesn't need to be a winner or even an agreement. In a healthy argument, two people are able to express their opinions, needs, resentments, or feelings without fear of violence, name-calling, or being hurt. Healthy arguing is an exchange of beliefs or feelings when there already exists a difference of opinion and possibly anger. Most important, a healthy argument needs to be limited to what is happening currently. It serves no purpose to bring up past incidents or mistakes as "ammunition" for the argument. Those who are arguing must also agree that if the argument becomes too intense, they can take a break to get their thoughts in order or calm down. Once they've done this, they can come back and continue their discussion. This must be agreed upon, however, so that one person doesn't walk away leaving the other feeling confused about what is happening. Today I will understand that I can have an argument without fighting. There doesn't need to be a winner, and we can agree that we disagree.

When I was in an abusive relationship, I was living in the cycle of violence. During the tension-building phase, there were signs that the situation was about to become violent or abusive. My abuser might have slammed doors, become silent, begun drinking or using drugs, or begun breaking things. I knew all too well what these signs meant. They, or others, meant that an incident was inevitable. Today I will think about what kind of behavior my abuser displayed during this phase. What sounds remind me of it? What actions do I remember? When did I know that something was about to happen? Today I will notice when any of these things happen in my new life. Do specific things remind me of this phase? Have I become more sensitive to the sound of breaking glass or a slamming door? I can remind myself that these things can happen all the time, and they're accidents. I will realize that they are not signs of impending violence, but I'll also allow myself to feel frightened. I can remind myself that my fear is caused by a memory and that I don't have to live in fear anymore. My memories will begin to lose their power.

Just as I can recall my abuser's behaviors during the tension-building phase, I can recall my own. How did I react when he was becoming irritated or angry? Did my heart beat faster, or did I shut down and stop talking? Did I go into another room to get away? Did I try to smooth things over? Did I get the children out of the house or try to get out myself? Today I will remember my own feelings and behaviors during this phase and compare them to how I react today when I'm frightened. Have I changed? Do I react differently now? Part of my healing is that I'll eventually become more normalized when I'm afraid. I might not necessarily fear for my life or fear I will be harmed as quickly as I used to. I know that it will take time to heal from these memories and incidents, but I'm confident that I will.

Sometimes people I meet, or people I already know, will ask me questions that make me feel uncomfortable. They might act as if they care, want to help me, or want me to confide in them, but to me it feels like they might just be nosy people. I don't have to answer any questions about my past or my present that I don't want to. I can choose whom I will confide in, whom I will share my experiences with, and whom I will trust. True friends are those who respect my privacy and do not ask questions about things that are none of their business. I can simply respond to nosy inquirers by telling them that I don't want to discuss my situation, I don't feel comfortable talking about it, or it's none of their business. Today I will respect my own privacy by choosing whom I trust.

➤ *Day 154*

Do I give up who I am or ignore my own needs to please others? During my abusive relationship I might have done so, thinking that pleasing my abuser would stop the abuse or prolong the time in between incidents. No matter what happened in my abusive relationship, today I will not give up my own needs to make other people happy. I will be more in touch with what I want, what my needs are, and how to say no to others. If I enjoy giving to others, I can decide when and how I will do this. If someone asks me a favor, I can decide whether or not I want to comply. Today I will practice breaking the habit of trying to make other people happy and focus instead on making myself happy.

➤ Day 155

If there are situations or circumstances in which I have no control, I will surrender. Surrender doesn't mean that I give up hope; it means that I accept the fact that I can't change an outcome. It means that I believe a situation will be taken care of, that the outcome will be for the best, and that I can let go of trying to force the outcome. When I practice surrender, I practice faith and the awareness that I can't fix everything. I might have to believe that other people are trustworthy or believe that God, my Spiritual Power, or whatever my spiritual entity is, will take care of me. Today I will realize that some things are out of my hands.

➤ Day 156

Today I will take care of what I have. I will not be preoccupied with what I want to have, but be grateful for what I do have. Even if I've not yet achieved my goals, or if my life isn't yet the way I want it to be, I will appreciate where I am now. Do I ignore responsibilities because I don't have what I want yet? Do I treat my belongings or surroundings badly because I want something different? Good things will come into my life more easily when I take care of and appreciate what I have now. Today I will focus on caring for what I've already gained and what I already possess, and I'll be grateful for wherever I am on my path of healing.

Do I wish I had more affection in my life? Do I see people in public places who are affectionate toward each other and wish I had that in my life? Perhaps there hasn't been any affection in my past relationships, or in my life, for that matter. If affection is what I want, I might have to practice being affectionate. I might have to think about reaching out to touch others or give them a hug. It might not be automatic for me to be an affectionate person, but today I will hug someone I love, for no reason at all. I can also choose to ask someone I love to give me a hug. Affection doesn't come naturally to everyone, and if I would like to have more physical affection in my life, I can let it begin with me.

Do I need a vacation? Have I been so concerned with making the right decisions, getting my life together, working, taking care of my family, or achieving my goals that I've forgotten to have fun? If I have the financial resources, I will begin planning a vacation. It might be elaborate, or it might not be. It might be a trip to another country, or it might be a trip to the beach. If taking a vacation is not possible right now, I will go to a travel agency and pick up brochures on places I would like to go. I can go to the library, search the Internet, or find books and maps of where I would like to travel. I can read about this place and put up pictures of it in my house. I can ride an exercise bike and pretend that I'm traveling through this place. Taking a vacation doesn't always have to cost a lot of money. If I don't have the money to travel or the time to do so, I can visualize myself in the places I've always wanted to go and enjoy my thoughts and plans of travel without spending anything or going any further than my dreams.

➤ Day 159

I've been learning how to say no and have practiced doing it. Today I will begin to say yes. I can look around me and imagine the things I want in my life. If I see a house or car that I would like to have, I will say, "That's for me!" If I see a couple in a loving relationship, and that's something I want in my life, I will say, "That's for me!" If I'm reading the "help wanted" ads and see a job I'd like to have, I will say, "That's for me!" Although I still need to know how to say no to what I don't want, today I will begin saying yes to what I do want.

➤ *Day 160*

Today I will practice tolerance. In the past, I may have been too tolerant, allowing someone else to walk all over me, abuse me, or mistreat me. In my healing, I may have become intolerant, not allowing for mistakes and having no patience at all. I will now pay attention to those areas of my life in which I can be more tolerant. When I begin to get upset or frustrated, I can take a deep breath and stop to think, *How important is this issue, and is it something that I must react to right now?* Do I have time to gather my thoughts, make a decision, and consider what benefit can be gained by reacting with anger or intolerance? How important would this singular issue be if it were to occur during an earthquake or other disaster? What are my priorities, and is it better for me to show a little more patience at this time? Today I will practice evaluating my tolerance level, and I'll learn to change it when necessary.

➤ *Day 161*

Today I will look at my spirituality. Do I have spiritual beliefs? Do I have a religion that comforts me? Do I have a church that I attend or would like to attend? Do my children have any spirituality in their lives? Do we pray together? Do we believe in God or a Spiritual Power? Today I will consider expanding our spiritual experience. If I already have spiritual beliefs, I will become more involved in them. I will volunteer in some way at my church, synagogue, group, or center. I can encourage my children to attend a youth program or camp. If I don't have a place to worship or don't feel a sense of spirituality, I may want to seek one out. I can attend any number of churches or groups and find one that fits my needs. If there are people who approach me and want more from me than I'm willing to give at this time, I can let them know that I'm looking around, but not willing to commit to anything yet. One of the most important things I can do for myself and my children is to expose us all to spiritual beliefs and allow ourselves the freedom to choose what makes sense for each of us.

I might feel that, in my new life, I have to stand on my own two feet, provide for my family, and take care of myself without help from anyone. While it's good to take responsibility for myself and my children, it's also okay for me to need help. It's okay for me to talk to trusted friends, ask their opinions, or just have them listen. It's okay for me to seek out professional advice, get therapy, or read self-help books. It's also okay for me to ask for a loan, for work, or for financial assistance. It's okay for me to need others in my life. There's a big difference between needing help and being needy. Needing help assumes that I'm contributing to my own situation in some way, but being needy means I want others to do everything for me. Today I will realize that when I need help, it's okay for me to ask for it.

In normal relationships, there may be low times as well as high times. It's unrealistic for me to expect every minute to be perfect and filled with happiness. There may be times when my partner and I disagree, want to do something separate from each other, want to spend time alone, or are simply in a bad mood. Relationships of any kind don't always have to be fun and exciting. Real life is about experiencing emotions of all kinds. We may experience sadness, frustration, anger, disappointment, depression, or any other feeling that isn't usually considered to be positive. These feelings are all part of life. Today I will accept that as long as I'm communicating my feelings, all of them are okay. I will allow others to have their own feelings too.

➤ Day 164

Today I will do something spontaneous. There might be many areas of my life that are planned and organized. While this kind of order is very important, so are activities that aren't planned. I can go to the movies, have a picnic lunch, or take my children for a drive to a park or the beach without having to plan it in advance. We might choose to eat dinner on a blanket on the floor or have a theme dinner where we get dressed up to match the menu. My life might have become too serious for too long. It is important for me to experience the childlike excitement of spontaneity once in a while, and today I will.

➤ *Day 165*

Today I will be willing to accept good things in my
life. I'm open to being happy, and I'm moving
forward with plans that feel good for me. I'm ready
to let go of pain and experience the joy of simply
being alive. I'm grateful to have come so far, and I
welcome kindness and love in my life now. Today I
will take a minute to thank myself for being open
to the good things life has to offer.

Do I ever think about acts of revenge? Do I wonder how I can get back at my abuser? Do I wish I could punish those who have hurt me? Today I will realize that revenge won't change the past, and moving forward in my life doesn't include revenge. If I feel that my abuser needs to be punished for what he's done, I can obtain an attorney, file charges, or seek legal advice. But if I'm thinking of pressing charges, I should look at my motives for doing so. Am I motivated by a sense of justice or revenge? Do I need to pursue this matter, or is it better to detach? Wanting to see people punished for things they've done wrong is normal, healthy, and legal. Wanting to "get back" at someone for hurting me is also normal but unnecessary. I can pursue my own healing and deal with my anger in other ways. I can also set an example for my children by showing them, and myself, that I can work through my feelings of being wronged by seeing a therapist, counselor, grief group, anger group, or Twelve Step group. Today I will try to better understand my motives when wanting to punish those who have hurt me.

➤ *Day 167*

Today I will accept that I'm doing the best I can. I will accept that, in the past, I tried to do what I thought was right at the time, and today I will accept that I'm still doing what I think is best. My best is all I can ask of myself for now. If I become judgmental or critical of my past actions, I will remember that I'm judging the past by what I know now. With each lesson learned and each step forward, I'm growing and becoming more knowledgeable than I was before. Today I will not judge my past behaviors. I will remember that how I handled situations then is not how I would handle them now. My decisions today would be very different than they would have been then, and I can give myself credit for that. I can appreciate what I've learned, and I'll continue to move forward.

When getting to know new people, I can ask them questions that will give me insight into their personalities. Instead of trusting that new people in my life are probably not abusive, I can ask them how they deal with their anger. I can ask them if they anger easily, what makes them angry, and how they handle their feelings when they become angry. Their answers will give me a clearer picture of what I might expect from them. It is okay to ask people about themselves when getting to know them. I don't have to wait for a situation to arise in order to see their behavior, although that may happen. I can ask up front, before a situation arises. Their answers will also ultimately let me know how honest they are with themselves and with me.

I have the right to be direct about what I'm thinking or feeling. I don't have to play games with people, expect them to read my mind, or communicate with looks or hints. I can speak directly and to the point about whatever I want or need to say. As long as I say what I mean without being mean, I always have the right to express my opinions, likes and dislikes, needs, and feelings. How the other person receives this information is up to him or her. I can't be responsible for how others feel about what I say. I can only do my best to express myself in the best way I can, with openness and directness.

Because of my experience with people who have tried to control me, do I ever find myself trying to control others? There are many ways that people try to control situations or other people. They can directly tell them what to do, or they can be subtle and manipulative. Trying to have control over other people doesn't achieve anything. The only person I can be responsible for—or control—is me. This does not mean I neglect my responsibilities to others as a parent, co-worker, or supervisor. Nor does it mean that I can't express my opinion when asked. It means that I refrain from trying to control how other people act, think, believe, or live. Today I will observe my own behavior and notice when I'm trying to control others. If I see myself doing this, I will stop it now. I can remember what it was like to be controlled and how much I resented it. I don't want others to feel that way about me. I will do whatever I can to stop this pattern in my own behavior.

➤ *Day 171*

I've learned about the cycle of violence, and today I will learn more about the dynamics that exist within the cycle. Learning about these elements will help me be more aware of what abusive relationships look and feel like, and also what to watch out for in the future. In an abusive relationship, the abuser might use intimidation. He might make his partner afraid by breaking things, threatening her, displaying weapons, hurting pets or the children, or using facial expressions or gestures. Today I will be more aware of times when people around me are trying to intimidate me. It is not okay with me, and I refuse to allow it in my life anymore.

In an abusive relationship, the abuser might use isolation. He might use jealousy and accuse his partner of being unfaithful. He might limit who she sees, where she goes, and what friends she has. He might move her far from her family and friends in an attempt to have total control over her. He might limit her time out of the home, placing unrealistic demands on her regarding when she must be home. He might create a scene in front of anyone she knows so they won't want to continue to be her friend. He might embarrass her in front of others in an attempt to stop her from developing new friendships. Today I will not allow anyone in my life to control me in this way. I can choose whom I will see, where I will go, how I will dress, and when I will return. I'm not isolated anymore, and I can have all the friends I wish to have. I can plan my own life without fear of anyone accusing me of doing something wrong. In the future, I will recognize abusive traits early on in anyone who tries to control me this way.

In abusive relationships, the abuser might use his "male privilege" as a form of control. He may define his partner's role as that of a submissive woman and not include her in any decisions. He might claim that he is the ruler, the king of the castle, the provider, or the breadwinner. He might treat her as a servant or slave. He might place unrealistic demands on her regarding how she should keep house or cook. Today I will not be put in a role created by someone else. I can be anything I want to be, including the breadwinner. I can make my own decisions about how I cook or keep house. In my house, I'm not a servant, and I have no ruler.

In abusive relationships, the abuser might use the children to control his partner. He might threaten to take the children away or tell his partner she'll never see them again. He might use the children to give her messages or threats. He might make the children act as witnesses while he hits her or otherwise abuses her. He might make her feel guilty about the children or threaten to hurt them if she doesn't obey him. He might threaten to harm her, or the children, if she ever tries to take them from him. Today I will not allow anyone to use my children against me. I will take the necessary steps to protect them and keep them safe, and I'll refuse to allow anyone to use them as weapons against me anymore.

In abusive relationships, the abuser might minimize or deny his abusive behavior. He might tell his partner that it's her fault or that she made him do it. He might tell her that if she were a better mother, wife, or person, none of it would be happening. He might deny that anything ever has happened. He might tell her that she is making a big deal out of nothing. Today I will not allow anyone to minimize what has happened to me. It *was* a big deal, and it wasn't my fault. Something was very wrong in my relationship with my abuser, and I will not settle for any type of relationship that reminds me of it, ever again.

In abusive relationships, the abuser might use emotional abuse to control his partner. He might criticize her, belittle her, call her names, tell her that no one else would want her, humiliate her in front of others, or make her feel guilty. He might tell her she's crazy, that it's all in her mind, or that no one will believe her. He might play mind games with her until she questions her own sanity. He might lie to her or create wild stories to confuse her. He might make excuses for his behavior that are unrealistic and ridiculous. Today I will not allow anyone to emotionally abuse me. I will not allow others to call me names or belittle me in any way. I was not crazy, nor am I crazy now. I have no interest in being around anyone who treats me in this manner, and I will not allow it ever again.

In an abusive relationship, the abuser might use finances to control his partner. He might stop her from looking for, getting, or keeping a job. He might keep control of the money so she has to ask him for it. He might take her money, put her on an allowance, or not tell her what their financial status is. He might put her in charge of the money and then blame her when there isn't enough to pay the bills. He might blame her when there isn't enough money for him to buy the things that he wants, or he might accuse her of overspending. He might tell her that she has no job skills and that no one will hire her. Today I will not allow anyone to control my finances except me. I will not share my financial information with other people when it's none of their business. I don't have to explain the way I spend money or why I make certain purchases. If I need help with financial planning or banking, I will ask for help from someone I trust. I will not allow anyone to use money to hold me hostage. I'm responsible and capable of handling money.

In an abusive relationship, the abuser might use threats to control his partner. He might make and carry out threats of violence. He might tell her that if she leaves, he will kill himself, her, or others. He might tell her that he'll report her to the authorities, leave her without anything, or include her in illegal acts. He might tell her she'll never make it without him or that no other man would want her. Today I will not listen to threats, but if I receive them, I will take the necessary steps to keep myself and my children safe. I do not have to listen to my abuser's threats or the threats of anyone else. I can use a middle person, or mediator, to communicate with my abuser safely. I do not have to subject myself to the threats of any abuser.

In an abusive relationship, the abuser might use sexual abuse to gain control. He might make his partner engage in sexual activities against her will or force her to have sex after a fight. He might sexually abuse their children and blame her or threaten her in order to keep it a secret. He might force her to have sex with him in front of the children or in front of others. Today I will promise not to allow anyone to force me to have sex or act sexually in any way that I don't consent to. I have the right to be loved and treated with respect, sexually and otherwise. I deserve it, and I will have it.

In abusive relationships, the abuser might use physical violence. He might use physical violence periodically. He might slap me or push me, prevent me from leaving the room, or grab my arm to prevent me from walking away. He may be physically violent all the time. He might knock me down, kick me, choke me, punch me, grab me, shake me, hit my head against the wall, trip me, rape me, throw me out the door, throw objects at me, hurt me with weapons, or act in other ways that cause me physical pain. Whatever the case may be, physical violence of any kind is illegal and wrong. Physical violence is not an option, an answer, or a solution. Today I will not allow anyone to harm me physically or in any other way. I have never deserved it, and I don't deserve it now. The abuse was never my fault, and I don't have to admit that I did anything wrong. If I consider the possibility of going back, or that I could have stayed with my abuser, I will remember the pain I felt. I will remember the incidents that mad me feel so alone, so hurt, so ashamed, and so worthless. I'm totally committed to living a life without abuse. I deserve it, and I will have it.

Now that I've learned about the dynamics of domestic violence and behaviors that are present in abusive relationships, I will become more aware of the elements in healthy, equal relationships. In equal relationships, two people experience fairness and compromise. They seek solutions to their conflicts and problems together. They're both willing to give and take and are accepting of change. As opposed to abusive relationships, in which one person makes the rules, an equal relationship is one in which both people agree on the rules and work together to make family decisions. They both decide how the work will be fairly divided in the home. When I practice making decisions on my own, before entering a new relationship, it better enables me to understand what I want. When I know what I want, I can enter into relationships in which my opinion matters, and I can contribute to making decisions.

➤ *Day 182*

In equal relationships, people make financial decisions together. In an abusive relationship, the abuser might have control of the finances, make all decisions about money, or become violent when discussing money. In equal relationships, both partners benefit from the financial situation. When I learn how to handle my own money before entering a new relationship, I'm better able to contribute to financial discussions. Today I will be sure that I learn to make financial decisions, plan a budget, open a bank account, balance my checkbook, write checks, pay bills, and take care of my family's money. If I don't know how to do these things, I will ask someone I trust to teach me. Learning how to handle money is an important and necessary part of being independent.

➤ *Day 183*

In equal relationships, people listen to each other so that each partner feels safe and comfortable. They allow each other the time and room to express their feelings, their wants and needs, and their thoughts without fear of violence or retaliation. Today I will practice listening to others without making negative comments. Even if I might not agree with what they say, I will practice listening and making positive comments that allow them to feel safe when talking to me. I will also find people in my life who do the same for me by letting me feel safe when I'm expressing myself. Being able to feel safe in a conversation, especially when talking about goals or personal information, is one of the most important elements in an equal relationship.

In equal relationships, people trust and support each other. They support each other's goals, feelings, activities, choices, and opinions. Even when they don't agree, they're still respectful of each other's right to have their own thoughts and plans. They're willing to discuss any conflicts that arise and compromise when necessary. In equal relationships, people support each other. Today I will support the people around me whom I love. I can listen to their hopes and dreams and encourage them in their challenges. I will also surround myself with people who do the same for me.

In equal relationships, people parent together. They share responsibilities for their children, and they provide nurturing, nonviolent role models for them. They talk about decisions together and work together to provide a safe and loving environment for their children. They discuss the discipline and rewards for their children together and provide consistency in these matters. Today I will be more in tune with what I want for my children, especially what kinds of discipline I agree with and what kinds of rewards seem fair to me. When I know what I want in my children's lives, I'll have a clearer picture of the kind of role model I want in any new relationship. When I'm dating new people, and when it's appropriate, I will discuss parenting with them. How do they parent their own children? What kind of discipline do they use? What rules do they think are fair in raising children? This information is very important when deciding whether to continue a new relationship. My children are my highest priority, and I will not make any decisions that will harm them.

In equal relationships, people trust and respect each other. They listen and value each other's opinions, and they are understanding and nonjudgmental. Even when they don't agree, they still respect the other person's right to his or her own thoughts and feelings. They trust each other and aren't suspicious or jealous. They don't make accusations or question each other about where they've been or what they've been doing. This information may be part of a conversation, but it is not part of an inquiry. Trust is very important in an equal relationship. Today I will practice trust. I will evaluate my trusting capabilities. Did I have good reason to distrust in the past? Am I ready to trust now? Have I become suspicious of other people's motives or behaviors? What would it take for me to trust someone again? I can be open and honest about my trust issues. I can take the risk of trusting again once I feel safe. I can look at relationships I've had throughout my life and think about the times my trust was betrayed. Am I ready to have someone in my life whom I can trust? Trust is a vital part of an equal relationship, and today I will be aware of how much I can give.

In equal relationships, people are honest and take responsibility for themselves. They tell the truth and don't lie, make excuses, or blame others for their behavior. They can admit their mistakes and admit when they're wrong. They communicate openly, directly, and honestly. They say what they mean without being mean. Equal relationships don't contain deceit and manipulation. Today I will make sure that I'm being honest in my life, and this includes not avoiding the truth. I will admit when I'm wrong or have made a mistake. I will not take the blame for others, but I will take responsibility for myself. Being able to be honest and accountable for myself is an essential part of an equal relationship.

➤ Day 188

Now that I know what types of behaviors are in abusive relationships and in equal relationships, I can evaluate my current relationships. Which ones do I think are abusive, and which ones do I feel are equal? Is there anything I can do to change those that are abusive? Is there some way I can help them to be more equal? Today I will take inventory of all my relationships and change what I can. I deserve to have equal relationships in my life, and I will practice being the kind of person whom I would want to have as a friend or mate.

➤ *Day 189*

Have I neglected my own needs lately? Am I getting enough sleep? Do I eat right? Do I have fun in my life? Today I will take care of me. I will plan to do something good for myself or change my current lifestyle so that I'm taking better care of myself. Is there something that I need to change in my schedule? Do I need to get up earlier to have some time to myself? Do I need to make sure there's more nutritious food in the house? Do I need to exercise in the evening instead of lying around? Today I will become more aware of my own needs and do what I can to meet them.

There may be some areas of my life about which I'm still in denial. Have I put off getting therapy or counseling, thinking I don't really need it? Have I procrastinated in finding counseling or a support group for my children, thinking that they're fine now and don't really need help as much as before? Perhaps I'm in denial about how serious my—or our—situation really was. What I've experienced, along with my children, was traumatic and life changing. I can't expect us to be fine just because we left. We most likely need help in order to heal from the past and move forward in our lives. Feelings that are left unspoken or unfelt may come back later to haunt us. Today I will look at any areas of my life that need my attention, and I will take action. I will come out of my denial and get on with the business of healing.

➤ Day 191

Today I will continue to let go of the people in my past with whom I no longer have anything in common. If these relationships aren't good for me, or remind me of painful experiences, I can let them go. I don't have to remain in relationships that don't serve any purpose in my new life. I can choose to say good-bye or simply stop calling. I'm now willing and capable of seeking out positive, equal relationships that are nurturing and good for me, and I deserve them.

➤ *Day 192*

Today I will notice the beauty in my life. Do I have new friends who love me and treat me with respect? Are my children doing well, and are they safe? Is my home free of violence? What does the weather look like outside? How often do I take the time to notice the beauty of my surroundings? Are flowers in bloom, or are autumn leaves falling to the ground? Is it snowing, or is the summer heat sending the neighborhood children to play in the water? No matter what season, there is beauty all around me. Today I will take notice and appreciate what I see. I'm grateful for each day and the goodness it brings. Even if I'm troubled or having problems, I can still find something of beauty for which to be grateful. Today I will make a list of five things for which I'm grateful and spend a few minutes being aware of them.

➤ *Day 193*

Each day is one more day of learning how to interact with other people. Treating people with kindness and allowing them to treat me the same is becoming second nature to me. I've learned what it's like to be free of abuse in my life, and I like it. I'm so deserving of happiness and joy. I deserve to be loved the way I've always wanted to be loved. Today I will realize how much kindness means to me and how fantastic my life is without violence and abuse. Life is good, and so am I.

Taking a time-out is not a punishment but a skill. A time-out is when someone needs to take a break from a situation in order to cool off, regroup, collect thoughts, or calm down. Taking a time-out can be a very useful tool for anyone, if used correctly. When taking a time-out, it's best for me to go for a walk and never to drive. I will not use drugs or alcohol when taking a time-out. I will go outside, in another room, or out for a walk and think about what has made me so angry. I will think about how I can best handle the situation and what I can say in a respectful, nonviolent manner. I will be gone no longer than one hour. When I return, I can let the other people involved know that I'm finished with my time-out and ready to continue our discussion. If I get too upset again, I can take another time-out. Taking a time-out is different from just leaving. All people involved must agree that it's okay to need a time-out and allow each other the freedom to take it. I can also encourage my children to take one when they become upset. Taking some time to cool down is okay, and it's a skill that we all can benefit from learning.

Sadly, many children are victims of domestic violence. Aside from physical or sexual abuse, there are many other ways that a child can be abused. In order to better parent my own children, today I will become more aware of the ways this can happen. An adult can abuse a child by using intimidation. An adult might make the child afraid by giving him or her dirty looks, making threatening actions or gestures, damaging the child's property, or using his or her physical size to frighten the child. Today I will be aware of how I relate to my children and whether or not I do any of these things. I will be aware of how I communicate with them so that I may be sure to give them the love and nurturing they need.

An adult can abuse a child by using isolation. The adult might not let the child have friends or attend school activities. The adult might tell the child that "silence is golden" or "children should be seen and not heard." The adult might talk about the child in front of her or him, but not include the child in the conversation. Today I will encourage my children to participate in group activities such as sports, drama, hobbies, or whatever their interests may be. I will do what I can to ensure that my children are included in conversations and encouraged to express their feelings and thoughts in a safe, nonthreatening environment.

➤ *Day 197*

An adult can abuse a child by making threats. He or she can threaten to hurt the child or the child's other parent, send the child away to another school, make comments like "you'll be the death of me" or "I could die for you, and this is how you thank me." The adult might threaten to destroy or give away the child's property, or harm a pet. He or she might threaten to remove what the child needs to survive, thereby creating a fear of dying within the child. Today I will not threaten my children, or any child. I will provide reasonable choices and consequences. I will include my children in the process of deciding what the consequences will be, and I'll make sure they know ahead of time what all the rules of the house are. I will provide a safe and nurturing parenting example.

An adult can abuse a child by using emotional abuse. The adult might call the child names, put her or him down, or play mind games. The adult might threaten to leave or might use the child as a confidant. The adult might tell the child that the family's problems are his or her fault, that the child is making the adult angry. The adult might tell the child that basic needs to survive will be met only if the child behaves a certain way. Today I will not confide my own problems or challenges to my children. I will tell my children when I've made a decision that affects them, but I won't share my process. I will respect my children's right to be children, and I won't expect them to handle the responsibilities or concerns of an adult. I will never call them names or belittle them.

Today I will parent my children to the best of my ability. I will respect their feelings, thoughts, opinions, and needs. I will treat them the way I want to be treated. Although they don't have the same rights or responsibilities as an adult, it's my job to prepare them for adulthood. This means helping them and encouraging them to make wise decisions, to accept the consequences of their choices, and to take responsibility for their actions. I can do this for my children by creating age-appropriate guidelines. For a three-year-old, the consequence of spilling milk might be helping to clean it up. For a seventeen-year-old, the consequence of staying out too late might be the loss of certain privileges. If I feel that I need help in my parenting, I can take parenting classes, speak to a therapist, or find parenting books or videos that can help me. The last thing I want is to raise children who will become batterers or victims of abuse. I can help prevent this with open communication, planning, and getting help when I need it. I will not limit my parenting skills by thinking that I know all there is to know about raising children. Today I will admit that there is always more to learn.

Today I will reassure my children that I'm doing the best I can and that I always have their best interests in mind. I will let them know that whatever happened in the past will not happen again. I will tell them that their safety is the most important thing to me, and I'll show them this by making wise choices in my relationships. My children might still be angry with me for having been in an abusive relationship. They might feel that I'm not capable of making wise choices, and they might still blame me for what happened in the past. I can find a way for them to either get counseling or attend a support group, and I can always ask them for their understanding and patience. I can admit that I've made mistakes in the past, but I've learned from them. I will reassure them that I will not allow abuse in our lives anymore.

Today I will be aware of when I make controlling statements. Statements that begin with "you should" or "you need to" or "you have to" are all statements that attempt to control others. I will remember how it felt to be controlled, and I will change the way I express my opinion or give advice. I will begin my statements with "you could" or "what has worked for me is" or "maybe you could consider," and by doing so, I'll be allowing others to make their own choices. When I tell others what they need to be doing or what they should do, I have a vested interest in the outcome. When I can detach enough to offer an opinion, the outcome is up to them. I will try not to control others, remembering that the only person I can control is me.

➤ Day 202

Today I will accept others for who they are. I don't have to try to change others in an attempt to make them better people. I don't have to focus on how they could be different or better. I can understand them as they are and be willing to let them be just that. I will accept that some people are nosy, critical, negative, self-centered, uncaring, or don't participate in relationships the same way I do. I can accept that people are not always the same as I am and that each of us is different. I will put forth an effort to be more understanding of others and not resent them because they don't behave the way I think they should. Today I will accept others for who and what they are.

➤ *Day 203*

When other people speak to me in ways that feel disrespectful or mean, I will tell them how I feel about it. I will tell them that what they've said has hurt my feelings or makes me feel sad or angry. I have the right to ask that others express themselves in ways that aren't hurtful. Today I will write down what my response might be if someone hurts my feelings or speaks to me in an uncomfortable tone of voice. When I learn appropriate ways to respond, I'm better able to stand up for myself and let others know how I'm feeling. I don't have to hold my feelings inside and allow verbal abuse to continue. I have the right to stand up for myself in all situations.

➤ *Day 204*

Today I will do one thing to expand my concept of myself. I will read a different kind of book than I usually read, sign up for a class I've only thought about taking, start writing poetry or the book I've been wanting to write, learn a new hobby or craft, try a new recipe, build something, plant flowers or a garden, or try anything that is new to me. I can expand my world by learning how to enjoy different activities. I don't have to stay locked in a regular routine or lifestyle. I can try new things, new ideas, and new avenues in my life. As I grow and change, so do my needs and desires.

Today I will be more aware of when I'm feeling vulnerable. Am I feeling confused or lost lately? Do I feel like I've opened myself up too much in a relationship? Am I worried about being judged or criticized? Am I feeling unsafe? When I'm feeling vulnerable, it's important to think about my good qualities. What things about me are worthy of noticing? What do I do well? What are some of my accomplishments? When I'm doubting myself or feeling vulnerable, I will take a minute to remember or make a list of all the good things about me. Am I a good friend? Am I a good parent? Am I a good person? We often feel vulnerable when we feel afraid that we can be hurt because we've opened our hearts to someone else. Today when I open my heart, I'm grateful that I'm willing to do so. I'm grateful that I'm willing to trust again, to share who I am and whom I want to become.

➤ *Day 206*

Have I placed limits on myself in my life? Do I find myself believing that I can only accomplish or achieve something to a certain degree? Do I find myself wishing that I could do more or that my life was better somehow? Today I will step outside of what I believe I can do and reach for what I want to do most. The one person who is stopping me from reaching my goal or changing my life might be me. Today I will believe I can change, and I will take the steps necessary to prove it to myself. It doesn't mean that change will happen overnight, but I can begin to reach a little further than I have before.

➤ *Day 207*

If I find myself obsessively wondering how things will change or how my problem might be solved, I will let it go. I don't always have to know *how* something will happen; I can simply believe that it will. I will encourage myself to believe that not everything is in my control, and I don't always have all the information about a situation. If I've done my best and taken the right actions, I will let go of having to know how things will work out. I will simply trust that they will.

✒ *Day 208*

Today I will enjoy my healing process. Even if I experience emotions that are difficult, I can still enjoy each step I take in creating a life that is free of abuse and violence. It might be necessary for me to relive painful memories or experiences in order to heal. I might find myself wondering why I have to go through such pain again. Each part of my healing process has a purpose, and today I will be glad that I can experience all of it. Pain is just as much a part of life as anything else. I will find comfort in knowing that to the same degree I experience my pain, I can also experience joy.

Today I will let go of my old negative beliefs and be open to positive new ideas. Do I believe that life is hard and unfair? Do I believe that people are not to be trusted? Do I believe that people care only about themselves? Do I believe that people are dishonest and only want to use me? Today I will be more aware of what I believe to be true, and I will let go of those beliefs that were created out of pain. I'm willing to trust and be trusted. I'm willing to love and be loved. I'm willing to let go of negative beliefs that came from being mistreated, and I'm willing to create new truths about my life. Today I will enjoy a new and more positive outlook. I can begin by having the awareness that there are exceptions to everything. Not all people are abusive, dishonest, manipulative, or self-centered. Not everything is unfair, one-sided, or misleading. There is goodness in the world, and I will be open to seeing it.

It takes a lot of strength to leave an abuser. It takes courage, direction, action, decision making, and most likely, asking for help. I might feel that I have to be strong all the time, because if I'm not, everything will fall apart. I might feel that I'm holding the world on my shoulders, and I can't let go for a moment or it will come crashing down around me. Today I will understand and realize that I don't have to be strong all the time. It is okay for me to feel vulnerable, needy, lonely, isolated, insecure, or any other feeling that I might view as weakness. I'm not weak if I feel any of these emotions; I am human. It's normal and reasonable to go through periods of time when I need to be hugged, want a shoulder to cry on, or need to feel more loved and appreciated. I can allow these other emotions to happen and understand that they're all part of me. My true strength comes from allowing myself to feel all my emotions and accept them for being part of who I am.

➤ Day 211

Today I will practice staying in the moment. I don't have to be preoccupied with future plans or worries, memories of the past, or what happened yesterday. I will learn how to be right here, right now. When I can focus on the moment at hand, I'll be better prepared for later and not so consumed with what was. The only thing that is real is right now. Staying in the moment may require some work on my part, but today I will understand the importance of remaining focused on my priorities.

Guilt adds nothing to my life and has no rewards. When I feel guilty, what have I gained? What are the results of guilt? What does guilt change? Nothing. Today I will remember that if I'm feeling guilty, it's because I'm a caring person. I'm probably remembering something I did in the past that I wish I hadn't done. My guilt can't go back and change anything. I will keep reassuring myself that I won't make the same mistake again or repeat the same behavior. I did the best I could at the time, and I made the best choices I thought I could make. Today might be different, and I might react differently. But when I feel guilty, it doesn't help me. Today I will not remain in guilt by making the choice to learn from past mistakes and go forward. Guilt has no place in my life, and I will not let it in.

Do I fear success? Is there something scary about having what I want? Am I afraid of what total happiness might feel like? Is being successful something I've never known? Today I will imagine myself being where I want to be in my life and having all the things I want to have. I imagine what it would feel like and what my life would look like. When I can imagine something, it is more likely to happen than if I believe it to be out of reach. What would my life be like without any crisis or turmoil? How would I feel if I suddenly found myself happy? Today I will let go of my fear of success and imagine what success would be like. Even if I've been treated like a failure in the past or someone has told me I will never amount to anything, today I will know that I deserve to be successful. I can achieve my goals, and because I have a desire for a better life, I'm successful right now.

In new relationships, I will participate in deciding when I will become intimate. I don't have to be pressured into anything I'm not ready for just to make someone else happy. I can be part of deciding how fast or slow the relationship will go. In equal relationships, two people can discuss these things and make the decision together. I can voice my opinions and express my needs without having to explain every detail. If I'm feeling that I'm not ready for a relationship to become intimate, I can say that I'm not ready. I don't have to share painful past experiences or give reasons why; I can talk about how I feel and what I need. If my new partner doesn't listen or has his own agenda and refuses to respect my needs, I will know that this relationship will not be good for me. I can tell when someone cares for me by sharing what I need and seeing how well he listens to me.

When I decide that my new relationship can become intimate, I will remember that my old abusive relationships are not part of this one. I can be open to being loved, to feeling good, and to being close to someone I care about. I do not have to share details of past relationships, because bringing up the past serves no purpose and doesn't add to my new love life. I can simply allow this relationship to evolve in its own way and be willing to take each moment as it comes. I will be open to receiving affection and attention that is non-threatening and nonabusive. I will allow someone who is important to me to hold me, compliment me, and treat me like I'm special, because I am.

I might have to remind myself that a new relationship is different from the abusive relationships I've had in the past. It is different, so I can act differently. I can open my heart to trusting, be open to feeling loved, and leave the past behind. If something reminds me of the past, I can let it go while understanding that it is most likely a reminder, but not an indication, of abuse. If the new person in my life raises his hand quickly, it doesn't necessarily mean he's going to hit me. If he raises his voice in conversation, it doesn't mean he's going to yell at me. If he slams the door, it doesn't mean he's angry with me or is going to hurt me. Sometimes nonviolent situations or incidents occur that would have frightened me while I was being abused. By themselves, they don't necessarily mean that I'm in danger now. I can notice these things and remind myself that they are probably reminders, and aren't always indications, of danger.

In a new intimate relationship, I can be honest about my needs. I don't have to settle for less when it comes to sex. I can talk about what I like and what feels good to me. In the past, I might have been told that I had to please my abuser, never paying attention to what felt good to me. I may have been forced to have sex when I didn't want to or to perform sexual acts that I didn't like. I may have settled for sex that didn't satisfy me because I wasn't permitted to ask for personal pleasure. In my new relationship, I can ask for what I want. If my partner doesn't respect this or doesn't allow me this, then perhaps this is not a relationship that is good for me. In equal relationships, both people have the right to be sexually satisfied and to talk to each other about their needs and desires.

➤ *Day 218*

If I don't know what I like when it comes to sex, or
making love, I can take some time to think about it.
I might not know what pleases me. I can think
about it, or I can ask my intimate partner to try
different things so I can find out. My healing
includes knowing what feels good, in all aspects of
my life, including my love life and sex life. I have
the right to feel fulfilled and satisfied, and I have
the right to ask for what I need. If I don't know, I
also have the right to ask for the support of my
partner as I find out what does satisfy me.

If I'm not ready for intimacy, I can choose to be celibate until I'm ready for sex. I can use my sexual energy in other creative ways. I can find hobbies, crafts, or other nonsexual activities in which I can be creative without being intimate. Perhaps I need more time to heal. Perhaps I need more time to prepare myself or to develop trust. I do not have to be intimate before I'm ready or have sex with someone just for the sake of having sex. I have the right—and it's also good for me—to wait until I meet someone who is safe, who is important to me, and with whom I feel comfortable before becoming intimate.

Am I using drugs or alcohol to change my feelings? Do I drink too much or use drugs to avoid or escape feelings that are uncomfortable? In my healing, I can understand that drugs and alcohol will not help me heal more quickly but might delay my healing. I don't have to use mind-altering substances to move forward or to deal with unpleasantness in my life. If I feel that these substances are helping me, I will look again. Do I really feel better while using them? What do they bring to my life? Do I really need them? I can also look at literature about alcoholism and drug abuse to find out if I have a problem. My healing is about recovering from abuse and anything else that's not good for me.

When I find myself feeling angry toward my family, I will look at the reasons why. Am I angry about something that recently happened or about things that have been going on for years? Do I blame my family members for my problems in any way? Do I resent them for things that have gone wrong in my life? Today I will take responsibility for how I respond to others. While I can't control how others treat me, I can control how I respond. No one makes me act or react a certain way. I'm the only person who can change the way I react. Today I will look at why I might be angry with my family and take the steps to deal with my anger. I can write about it, talk to my therapist, talk to a trusted friend, confront my family members, or send them letters. I don't have to hold my feelings inside when there are ways to let go of my anger.

➤ Day 222

Is there anything about accomplishing my goals that scares me? Am I afraid that it would make my life so different that I wouldn't know how to act? Do I feel that I couldn't handle success or a change for the better? I may be so used to feeling like a victim or being mistreated that the idea of being in control of my own life seems frightening. Today I will make a list of things that scare me about positive change. Would I have more money to handle? Would I have to be more responsible? Would I have to interact differently with other people? Would I have to let go of talking about being abused or reliving the details of my abuse? I will think about what might be scaring me and write about it. Even if some of my thoughts don't make sense now, I will write them down. Moving forward is important to me, and this is part of coming to a place where it can happen more easily.

➤ *Day 223*

Today I will solve the problems of today. I might have become so focused on solving all the problems in my life that I haven't noticed the little problems that arise each day. Do I have anything that needs to be completed or resolved today? I will take a moment each day and work on what I need to do just for that day. Even though solving long-term problems is necessary, so is solving the smaller daily problems. Not allowing things to pile up keeps me from feeling overwhelmed. Today I will pay attention to what needs to be solved today.

Today I will take a look at gossip. How do I feel when other people gossip about me? Does it hurt me? Does it make me sad? Do I get angry? Do I get involved in gossiping about others? Gossip serves no purpose, is cruel, and brings nothing but pain and sadness. Today I will begin to let go of the need to maliciously talk about others. If I find myself doing so, I will stop and excuse myself from the conversation. I don't want to be the topic of gossip, so I won't gossip about others.

Loving others unconditionally doesn't mean allowing myself to be hurt. If someone I love unconditionally is taking my kindness or generosity for granted, I will reevaluate that relationship. I can let it go, move on, or confront the other person. When I love people unconditionally, it means that I don't try to change them, make them think the same way I do, wish they were something they're not, or love them only when they behave a certain way. Unconditional love means that I accept others for who they are and allow them the space to grow in their own way. Being loved without conditions doesn't give someone the right to hurt others.

When I love others, I accept their needs, desires, and thoughts. I can accept that they might not want to spend every free minute with me. I can understand that they might want or need to have time to themselves, or that they have other responsibilities. I accept—which doesn't mean I have to like—that they might choose to do something with their time besides spend it with me. When I begin to love in healthy ways, I might feel that I can't get enough love. I might appreciate a person so much that I want to spend all my time with him or her. Today I will understand that in healthy relationships, we sometimes need to spend time away from each other. When I spend time taking care of my responsibilities, or away from my new love interest, it doesn't mean our relationship isn't special or important to me. It means that I'm living my life now as a healthy adult, capable of setting priorities and allowing others to do the same.

➤ Day 227

Loving others doesn't mean that I love them only when it's convenient for me. I can still love other people when they have ideas, agendas, or plans that are different from mine. If I'm in the mood to be affectionate, it doesn't necessarily mean that they are too. If I'm in the mood to have an important discussion, they might not want to have one at that time. If I feel like joking or teasing, they might be in a more serious mood. When I emotionally or intellectually connect with another person, it is exciting and stimulating. When I accept and allow others to be in a different mood than I am, or have different communication needs than I do, it is respectful and loving. Healthy communication is when two people can express their thoughts and needs without fear of not being loved if they do.

Do I find myself obsessing about a new relationship, whether it's real or a fantasy? Do I become easily distracted or neglect daily responsibilities because of my daydreaming? Am I consumed with planning my future and thinking about all the details? Do I constantly think about what my relationship will be like, planning every aspect of each event, conversation, or situation? Being aware of positive changes I'd like to see in my life and where I'd like to be in the future is normal and a sign of positive emotional healing. Being preoccupied with every little detail is not. Planning is healthy; obsessing is not. Setting goals is healthy; procrastinating is not. Today I will realize when I'm spending too much time with future thoughts and bring myself back into the moment. After all, I can't get to the future unless I take care of the details in my life today.

I should not be expected to always know what someone else is thinking. Do I find myself wondering if I've hurt other people's feelings or made them angry by something I've said or done? Are they acting in ways that remind me of my abuser, making me unsure of what they're thinking? I don't have to assume the worst or feel insecure about how others might be feeling about me. If I'm wondering how other people are feeling, I can ask them. When I take a chance by asking others how they feel or whether I've done something to upset them, I show courage by communicating in healthy ways. It's a waste of time to spend hours, days, or weeks wondering what I might have done wrong or belittling myself for what I think I did. All I have to do is ask and either deal with the problem or find out that I haven't done anything wrong in the first place. Because of past relationships, I might let myself become overcome with guilt, thinking that I've done something wrong. Today I will face these situations head-on instead of letting them build up and go unresolved.

➤ *Day 230*

Today I'm willing to let go of crisis. There has been so much of it in my past that a life without it may seem strange. It may seem boring or uneventful, and I might feel like something is missing. The fact is, the thing that's missing is unnecessary drama, crisis, or disruption. Today I will notice when I'm making a decision that will bring about crises and problems. Is this a decision I really need to make now? Is this something that can be avoided until later? Unless my safety is at risk, I don't have to make choices that will result in turmoil. A boring life is not necessarily without reward. I can learn to live calmly, peacefully, and without the dramatic ups and downs of the past. Today I will take a deep breath and appreciate what it feels like to relax and enjoy a life without crisis.

➤ Day 231

Do I have trouble believing that I'm worthy of being loved? How do I feel when other people give me compliments? Do I feel embarrassed? Do I feel like they want something from me? Do I feel like they're lying? As uncomfortable as it might be, when I receive a compliment, I will respond by saying thank you. As difficult as it might be to imagine, there are things about me that other people like or appreciate. When they show me kindness by acknowledging my good qualities, I can thank them. When I discount or disagree with a compliment someone has paid me, I'm basically saying, "You're wrong." Refusing a compliment doesn't make me a better person, more attractive, or more humble. When I can thank people for their sincere acknowledgment, it shows that I have self-confidence and that I'm proud of who I am. Today I will begin to thank people when they pay me compliments.

Do I give others the compliments they deserve? Do I feel shy or uncomfortable when it comes to telling them that I appreciate them or notice their good qualities? If I say nothing, they may never know how I feel or never learn to recognize their positive attributes. Today I will pay closer attention to the good qualities in others and compliment them on what I see. I will notice when my children accomplish a task and tell them they did a good job. If they make a good choice, I will tell them so. If they're working hard in school, I will acknowledge them for it. I will be aware of when a friend looks especially nice or chooses a pleasant fragrance, and I will tell her or him. If I appreciate that someone expresses himself or herself well, offers good advice, has good taste, or possesses any other quality that I admire, I will tell that person so without expecting anything in return.

Do I offer my thanks or appreciation when other people show me kindness or do me favors? Do I feel embarrassed to thank them or acknowledge them for their generosity? Even if a favor is one that I might have difficulty repaying, I can still say thank you. If I'm able, I can buy a thank-you card or gift, write a little note, or let them know I will be there if they ever need a favor. Today I will be happy to show my appreciation for the things that others do for me. I don't need to feel embarrassed if I need their help or need to ask a favor. I'm a good and valuable person, worthy of assistance when I need it, and today I will thank others and show my appreciation for the times they are there when I need them.

➤ Day 234

Today I will look at the worries in my life. I will revisit how I dealt with worries in the past, then look at how I deal with them now. Do I worry less? Do my worries seem less intense or less dramatic? Have I changed my behavior when I'm worried? Am I quicker to take action or make decisions? Has anything changed in the past few months in the way I handle my worries or what I do about them? I can evaluate my worrying process and make any changes I need to make. I will remember that worrying isn't a solution, doesn't change an outcome, and doesn't make a problem go away. I can be concerned about a situation without being consumed with worry. I can write about my worry and put it in a worry box, hang it on my worry wall, pray about it, talk to a trusted friend or therapist about it, or do whatever works best to help me let go of unnecessary worry.

Do I find myself feeling hypersensitive or easily upset by the actions of others, simply because they remind me of how I was treated in the past? Perhaps I had an abusive employer who was overly controlling or demanding. I might now find myself in a new job where my employer requires certain duties of me, which reminds me of the way I felt when I was controlled at my previous job. Instead of reacting by becoming angry or refusing to comply, I can recognize what is happening and act appropriately. Is my new employer abusive? Is she or he placing unreasonable demands on me? Is this another situation that needs to be changed? Or is it simply a reminder of my past that I can recognize, understand to be different, and let go of? Making a transition from an abusive situation to a non-abusive situation is not only difficult, but it also requires my full attention. While there may be some similarities between the two situations, the motives and reasons are different. Having this awareness helps me better know whether to leave a situation or to acknowledge it as a reminder and adjust.

➤ *Day 236*

Today I will realize when I'm feeling stuck. Am I feeling depressed or low on energy? Do I find it hard to get going every day? Do I lack motivation? Are my responsibilities piling up while I accomplish less? I can begin to solve the problem by making a list of what I need to do today. If my list is too overwhelming, I can break down each task into smaller ones. I might need to force myself to do one thing today, then two things tomorrow. Once I begin to feel a sense of accomplishment, my tasks will become easier. It is normal to feel depressed once in a while, but allowing it to continue is damaging to my growth and self-worth. I need to keep looking at the positive things in my life to feel motivated toward achieving more. What are the things for which I'm grateful? What good things have happened to me in the past few months? I might even need to imagine how things could be worse in order to fully appreciate how good they really are. Taking care of myself includes completing my daily responsibilities and taking the time to notice the good things in my life.

When it comes to my feelings about the past, I might have found comfort in telling myself that I did the best I could at the time. Knowing this probably helped me get through some tough times and deal with my feelings of guilt. Today, when I find myself feeling guilty about something I've done, I can still remind myself that I'm doing the best I can. With all my knowledge, growth, healing, and willingness, I will still make mistakes. I'm not perfect, nor do I strive to be. I'm doing the best I can do, day by day. Today I will remind myself of this anytime I feel bad about something I've said or done.

➤ *Day 238*

Today I will live the day to its fullest. I will not put it on hold while waiting for something that *might* happen. I will not wait by the phone in hope that someone might call. I will not stay home in hope that someone might stop by. I will make plans and use each minute doing something important to me. Even if my plans are to rest, watch a movie, read, shop for groceries, or take a nap, I will be choosing to do something I want to do with my time. I don't have to spend one precious moment of my life waiting for what *might* happen.

➤ *Day 239*

Today I will do something that makes me laugh. Whether it's watching a funny movie, playing a game with my children or friends, reading a humorous book, going to an amusement park, or finding a way to just be silly, I will get in touch with my playful side and have fun. A balanced life means experiencing laughter along with being serious. Not only am I willing to be a responsible adult, but I'm also willing to laugh, have fun, be playful, be childlike, and enjoy the simplest of pleasures. Today I will create or participate in one activity that makes me laugh out loud.

Do I look at certain situations and read more into them than is really there? Do I assume that other people are feeling a certain way, only to discover that I am wrong? Do I make assumptions about situations, only to find out that their circumstances are totally different from what I had thought? My imagination might go wild when I try to read into others' behavior. In an abusive relationship, my imagination might have kept me safe. I most likely learned how to figure out what my abuser was thinking or planning, and because I could read his behavior so well I was usually right. In my life without abuse, however, I might not always correctly assume what others are thinking. I don't have to second-guess their thoughts or actions, nor do I have to prepare for the worst. I can accept situations at face value and refrain from reading into them. If I'm unsure about something, I can ask. If I'm unable to ask, I will refrain from projecting my own fears and anxiety.

When I enter into a new relationship that is not abusive, my children might resent it. They might be afraid that the abuse will happen again. They might express their anger or resentment toward my new relationship, perhaps even by telling me all the things they don't like about my new partner. They might refuse to meet the new person, speak to him, or be included in our plans. Once I evaluate the relationship to be sure that it is not abusive, the most important thing I can do is give my children the time they need to get used to this new person. By giving them the time they need and not asking that they accept him on my terms, I'm showing them that I respect their feelings and boundaries. Today I will allow my children the room they need to feel safe in any new relationship.

➤ *Day 242*

My children might not accept a new relationship quickly. They might be critical, skeptical, and unsure of any new relationship I may have. In the past they probably felt my choices weren't in our best interest, and they are most likely afraid I will make the same mistakes. The first things I must consider are whether enough time has passed in order for me to heal from previous abuse and whether I have sought professional help for myself and my children. Have I made sure that we've all had the opportunity to talk about the abuse and had the chance to heal? If I'm confident that I've done so, and I'm comfortable about being in a new relationship, I must realize that just because I'm ready doesn't mean that my children are ready. I can encourage them to talk about their feelings, and I will listen to them. I will not argue with them, try to change their minds, or make them feel that they're wrong. I can reassure them that I've grown, that I realize my mistakes from the past, and, most important, that I will not make any changes that affect all of us until we all are ready. I deserve a safe and loving nonabusive relationship, but I must also listen to the feelings and fears of my children.

Even though I know how important it is to listen to and accept the feelings and fears of my children, I'm still responsible for making the decisions that I feel are best for us as a family. I can let my children, or any concerned friend or family member, know that I plan to move slowly before making any decisions and that I'm carefully evaluating everything before doing so. If they express reservations or concerns, I can remind them that their opinions matter to me, and, after listening to them, I will make the decision I feel is right. I am the adult, parent, grown-up, and head of our family. I will be the one to make the choices, rules, agendas, or plans that I believe will be in our best interest. Today I will remind myself of this and not allow others to make decisions for me.

If my children are behaving in ways that I feel are unreasonable or are coming from anger, I can choose to seek professional help for them. It is quite possible that my new relationship is triggering their memories of the past. Their behavior might not be about a new relationship at all, but about their memories of past abuse. If this is the case, it might seem that no one will be good enough for them, earn their trust, or be worthy of me. Seeing a therapist would probably be best for them, giving them the opportunity to confide in someone else besides me. Today I will not expect my children to like or accept someone just because I do. I can find a therapist who can work with them to continue their healing, and I can give them the time they need to do so. If they make comments or judgments about my new relationship that are unrealistic, I will remind myself that this anger is probably not about what is happening right now, but about what has happened in the past.

Moving too fast in a relationship is a warning sign, for myself or anyone else who cares for me. If I feel this happening, I will slow down the progress of the relationship and give myself the time I need to make wise choices and decisions. I will also be aware of when my new romantic interest tries to move too fast or encourages me to move too fast. Today I will take things slowly, giving myself the time I need to develop and practice new communication and relationship skills. If relationships are to be successful and lasting, taking things slowly is the best decision to make. If I truly care for someone, I will want to care for and nurture the relationship, not go full steam ahead. I will wait at least one year before moving in with someone, having someone move in with me, or getting married. I will take the time to look at where I'm going and evaluate my every step to make sure it's where I want to go.

Today I will review the signs that tell me when a relationship is becoming abusive. Is my partner trying to control me in any way? Does he tell me how to dress, fix my hair or makeup, walk, or act? Does he tell me how to behave in front of others? Does he tell me how to discipline my children? Does he try to set rules in my house? Does he seem bothered when I express my opinions? Does he seem insecure and get jealous easily? Does he think that hitting a woman is okay if she deserves it? Any or all of these are warning signs that this relationship could become abusive. If I suspect that a new relationship is or will become abusive, I will end it. I will not criticize myself if this happens, but be glad that I recognized it and did something about it. I will not make excuses for this person, nor will I try to convince myself that it might be different this time. I refuse to be abused anymore, and when I suspect it might happen, I will stop it. I would rather be without a relationship in my life than be abused again.

➤ *Day 247*

Today I will be grateful for where I am now. My life might not be perfect, and I might not have achieved the goals I thought I would have by now. I might not be living the kind of life I thought I would be or want to be, but I'm grateful for this day, right now, and the fact that I've made a commitment to myself to live a life in which I'm treated with respect and dignity. I will use this day as a gift, one that I've given myself because I deserve it. I will use this day to be glad for all I've accomplished. I'm deserving, worthy, and valuable. I'm a lovable person, and today I thank the person who helped me understand this: me.

➤ *Day 248*

Today I will give myself flowers. I can either call the florist and have them delivered to myself or get them at the grocery store, a gift shop, or a corner flower stand. I can even pick wildflowers from a field. However I go about it, I will give myself flowers today. My bouquet can be extravagant, or it can be simple. The card will read, "To [my name], for loving me and for all you've done for me." I don't have to sign it if I don't want to, but I will know that the flowers are from me. I don't have to wait for someone else to send me flowers to feel special. I can give myself something nice anytime I think of it. After all, I deserve it.

Today I will look at myself in the mirror and take a good look. Does my outside match my inside? Do I look like I want to look? Is there something that I want to change? Would I like a new haircut? Would I like to change the way I put on my makeup? Would I like to try a different hair color? Do I need some new clothes? Does my weight need to change? Do I want different glasses? Do I want to get contact lenses? When I look in the mirror, I will decide if I'm happy with the way I look, and I will make any changes I feel like making. When I'm happy about my looks, it's easier for me to feel more confident about myself. If I like the way I look already, I will look in the mirror and appreciate how good I look. If I like what I see, or if I do when I make the changes I want to make, I can say out loud, "I'm so good-looking" or "I'm so gorgeous" or "I'm so successful." Today I will change my appearance if I desire, and I will give myself the compliments I deserve.

➤ *Day 250*

After leaving the world of being abused, I've made many changes in myself. Today I will take a good look at my surroundings. Do they make it look like I live here? Do they represent who I am? Are there changes that I've been wanting to make? Do I want new pictures on the walls, different furniture, or different rugs? Would I like to move things around? Today I will focus on my home and make any changes I want to make. Perhaps I could trade bedrooms with someone else in the house. Perhaps I've been wanting to move to a different house. I've made changes in myself, emotionally and mentally, and these changes were oftentimes extremely difficult. The one thing that never changes is the fact that things change. Today, if I'm bored or unhappy with the way things look in my home or if I need a new living situation, I will begin making those changes.

➤ Day 251

Today I will plant something. Have I been wanting to learn about gardening? Do I already know how to plant flowers or grow vegetables? I will learn about different kinds of plants and trees, whatever I'm interested in growing. I will find out what kind of soil, light, and nutrients they need, and I will plant whatever I desire. I might have been wanting flowers, a winter garden, herbs, or a fruit tree. I've been spending a lot of time growing, and today I will switch the focus from myself by planting something, nurturing it, and helping it grow, as others have done for me.

I might not always feel the way I think I'm supposed to feel. Has something happened that I think should make me feel sad, but I don't? Has something happened that would make most people happy, but I don't feel that way? I might not have the reaction that I think I should be having, but it doesn't mean that something is wrong with me. Some circumstances might be individual to me and affect the way I feel. If I've been in the employ of someone who seemed abusive or controlling, and I've lost my job, I might wonder why I don't feel upset. The fact is, leaving an abuser is a positive step. I can overlook the fact that I lost my job and feel excited that I'm no longer being abused. When most people set boundaries or limits, they often feel proud that they have done so. I might not necessarily feel happy or proud, but upset that I was put in that position. Just because I don't feel the way I think I should feel, it doesn't mean that I've made a mistake, been misunderstood, or am wrong. Today I will be glad that I'm aware of my feelings, no matter what they are.

➤ *Day 253*

Today I will look ahead with a positive attitude. There may have been times when I was so preoccupied with my problems or negative feelings that I lost sight of how it feels to be optimistic. Even though it's part of life to experience "down" times or conflicts, I can still look ahead with a sense of anticipation. I will remember that I'm worthy of goodness and that wonderful things can come my way. Today I will plan on having positive things happen to me. I'm confident that if I'm open to them, they will come my way.

Do I still find myself wishing that my friends or acquaintances would change? Do I tell myself that I accept them as they are, but have a hidden agenda for how I might change them? Do I make subtle remarks or statements meant to manipulate them? Today I will realize and accept the fact that I can't change others. If they have asked me for help, I will ask myself if helping them is something for which I'm responsible. Have I been asked to do a simple favor for a friend, or is someone asking me to do the impossible? I can't change others, nor do I want to try. I don't have to take it upon myself to alter or improve someone else's behavior. The only person I need to worry about is me. Today I will focus on improving my own behavior and making the changes I need to make, and I'll let others do the same for themselves.

➤ *Day 255*

Keeping balance in my life might be difficult at times. I might be in a situation in which I have to work more than I'd like. Perhaps I'm spending time with my children but not finding enough time for myself. Today I will look at how I spend my time and begin to bring more balance into it. How can I plan my activities so I can spend ten more minutes a day on myself? Is there a way that someone could help me with my children so I can attend a support group or class that I want to take? Is there a way that I can arrange my work schedule so I have more time to spend with my family? I always have choices, and today I will choose to find ways of balancing my life.

Have I been taking care of my health? How long has it been since I've had a checkup or a physical exam? Do I eat food that's good for me? Do I exercise? Do I get enough rest? Today I will take care of my health and realize that it's a basic need. I must take care of my basic needs first if I'm to meet any of my other needs. My health must come first, and today I will make a promise to take care of myself.

Has my perception of danger changed since I left my abuser? Do I now have a clearer picture of what is dangerous and what is safe? Some situations are obviously dangerous, such as driving on the wrong side of the road, sitting too close to a fire, or leaving a young child unattended. But what about the things that weren't so clear to me in the past? How do I view danger now? Have my senses become more aware? Do I wonder how I could have lived in an abusive relationship and not been more afraid? Do I question how I could have stayed with someone who hurt me or threatened to hurt me? It has probably taken a lot of practice, but I view danger differently than before. This shows me that I'm growing and healing. I don't put myself in the same types of situations and try to convince myself that they're not so bad. Today I'm so much more aware of when I'm safe and when I'm not.

➤ Day 258

I've developed many skills that can help me process a difficult situation. I can remember to breathe, write in my journal, talk to my therapist, or put a note on my worry wall. I can write a letter to someone with whom I'm angry or upset without having to send it. I can express myself honestly and directly. I can set boundaries much more easily than before, and I can stick to them. Today I will be grateful for all the tools I've been given. If I haven't remembered them until now, I can begin to use them. Sometimes the most difficult task is working through my feelings about a situation, not deciding what I can do to change it.

➤ *Day 259*

Today I will write about my spiritual beliefs. Am I a religious person? Am I an agnostic or an atheist? Do I have a Spiritual Power in my life? Is there something or someone that I believe in, that helps me and comforts me through life's challenges? Today I will write about my beliefs and the part they play in my life. Do I have beliefs that have helped me and not talked to my children about them? Have I given my children the opportunity to develop their own spiritual beliefs? Perhaps now is a good time to talk about spirituality with them. I can listen to my children when they express their opinions or ask questions about spirituality. I won't try to force them to believe what I do. I can offer to take them to the church of their choice and allow them to grow in their faith in their own way.

Today I will notice how I react in normal and healthy confrontations. When I find myself in a situation in which I need to stand up for my beliefs or express myself, how do I feel? Does my heart beat faster? Do I feel nervous? Do I want to run away? Do I feel confident and self-assured? Do I communicate using "I" statements? If I think that I need to improve how I handle myself during confrontations, when possible, I will plan what I want to say. I can think ahead to a forthcoming conversation, know ahead of time what I want to say, and practice saying it to myself or to a trusted friend. If I plan ahead, I'm usually better equipped to communicate my feelings and thoughts.

Having a social life or a circle of friends is important to my healing. When I look at my social life, do I find it satisfying? Do I feel that I spend time with people I like while doing things I enjoy? Do I have different friends with whom I can talk or spend time? If I'm happy with this area of my life, it proves that I've come a long way. I'm able to choose my own friends without someone else telling me whom I can see and whom I can't. If I'm not happy, today I will reach out to make a friend. Perhaps there is someone at work, at my church, in my support group, or in my neighborhood whom I enjoy talking to on occasion. I can invite this person to lunch or to have coffee. I can find out more about this person and decide whether I'd like to see him or her socially. We can go to a movie, go out to dinner, or take our children to the park. Reaching out and making friends helps me break free of old isolation patterns and learn how to communicate in healthy ways. I'm free to meet new people and spend time with them, simply for the sake of having a new friend.

What are my expectations for my life? I've probably made and focused on short-term goals so far. What are the long-term goals I have for myself? Where do I see myself in a year, or five years, or even ten years? Do I want to have accomplished certain things or live a specific lifestyle? When I become clear on how I see myself in the future, it helps me in current relationships. When choosing a new relationship, or becoming involved with someone with whom I'd like to spend my life, it's important to know if we share the same goals and dreams for our future. Having these ideas in mind doesn't mean that I can't be flexible in my plans. It means that I have some kind of picture of what I want in my life. When I was in an abusive relationship, I might not have had future goals. Everything might have been clouded and confusing. In my life now, I want to understand myself well enough to plan for my future. Today I will write about how I would like my life to be. I will write about the type of house I'd like, where I'd like to live, what I'd like to be doing, and what my lifestyle might be like. Having a plan and knowing myself better will help me in my healing and in my relationships.

Today I will look at relationships that are incomplete. Is there someone in my life, in my family, or in my past with whom I need to communicate? Have I needed to tell someone something or have a confrontation, but have been waiting until I was ready or until I was stronger? Perhaps now is the time. I can make a list of one person or many people and write down what it is I need to say to them. I will call them and make arrangements to see them, or I can write them a letter. Completing relationships and finding closure is important to my personal growth. If I feel the need to say things to my abuser that I've been wanting to say, I don't have to see him in person. I can write down my thoughts or feelings, or tell them to my therapist. The most important thing I can do is find a way to bring my feelings out in the open. Holding them inside is no longer an option. Holding them inside stops me from moving forward in my life.

Have I become so used to sharing personal information about myself that I forget that others might not want to do the same? Do I try to have conversations with others that might be too personal for them? Today I will be more aware of when I'm prying into the lives of others. Perhaps they aren't used to discussing deep feelings or personal information. I will respect their privacy and the fact that they might be in a different place than I am. I can have conversations with others that don't have to be related to healing or recovery. I can learn how to talk about simple and unimportant matters without having to analyze personal issues. Although many of my experiences have been serious, I don't always have to be serious. I can have conversations with others that aren't about personal issues.

➤ Day 265

Today I will enjoy this day for exactly what it is: a day in my life. This is a day that I'm living for myself and not someone else. I probably don't have to plan any big changes today, finish a huge project, or make any major decisions. I can simply enjoy the weather and each part of the day. I can stop and notice the morning, afternoon, and evening; I can be aware of when I'm hungry or when I'm tired. I can take a moment to look in the mirror or watch my children. Today I will soak in everything about this day. I am glad to be alive. I'm glad to be in a place where no one is treating me badly. I'm glad for this day I've been given. I can say thank you to myself for being willing to be here.

Somewhere, right now, there's a woman or a man who is being battered, hit, yelled at, threatened, mistreated, or belittled. Today, while I'm grateful that it's not happening to me, I can have compassion for others. Instead of judging them for not leaving or deciding to do something about it, I will remember where I came from and what they must be feeling. I can remember the pain of not knowing I had a choice. I can remember the confusion of not knowing what to do. I can recall what it felt like to feel hurt and trapped. When I remember all this, it makes today seem all that much better. Considering the pain that others are going through helps me be a compassionate person, not in a codependent way, but in a caring way. It is normal and okay to feel bad for others who haven't yet found their way. If it helps me, I can say a prayer for them. If it helps me, I can take advocate training and volunteer at the local shelter. If it helps me, I can light a candle for them. If it helps me, I can understand that we are each on our own path, and we each have to find our way in our own time. Today I'm grateful that my time came when it did.

➤ *Day 267*

An excuse is nothing more than an excuse. In the past, I was probably a master at excuses. After all, I had learned from one of the best: my abuser. Today I don't have to make excuses anymore. I don't have to explain to others why I do certain things or make certain decisions. If I choose to do so, I can give them reasons, but I don't have to make up excuses. I also don't have to accept the excuses of others. I can be open-minded enough to listen to reason, but I don't have to buy into their feeble excuses. Excuses don't make much sense and are usually there to cover the truth. Today I will accept nothing less than the truth, and in truth there's no room for excuses.

When things happen in my life, I might find myself wondering, why me? What have I done to deserve this? Why am I being punished? Sometimes I don't get to know *why* something has happened; I must accept that it just did. Just like a child who asks why the sky is blue, I must be satisfied with the answer "it just is." I might not like it when I don't have enough details to satisfy my curiosity, but I can't always have them. Today I will accept that things happen over which I have no control, and there's no apparent reason why they did. Although I can take the necessary steps to improve my situation, the reality is that I may never know why some things happen. Sometimes, they just do.

There might be people in my life who still don't trust me because of decisions I made in the past. I might not have known how to make decisions that were in the best interest of myself or others. Even though I've come a long way in my healing, I still might not have earned the trust that I deserve. Today I will understand what it means to trust myself. Am I happy with the decisions that I'm now able to make? Do I find that I consider outcomes before making important decisions? Do my actions prove that I'm acting more responsibly than before? Even though I might not have established the trust of those close to me, I will still trust myself to do the best I can. If others are questioning the way I handle situations or trying to advise me to do otherwise, I will listen to my own voice with confidence. I trust that I've learned from past mistakes, and I handle things differently now. In time, others will come to trust me. But for now, I will understand the importance of trusting myself without needing their approval.

➤ *Day 270*

I can decide on the path I will take without having to please others in the process. In abusive relationships, I learned how to plan my activities and schedule my time around the needs of my abuser. Today I will take charge of my own life and make my plans according to what I want. If I set goals for myself, it feels good to know that I've set them based on what I want, not what someone else wants. Even though I can listen to the opinions or feelings of others, I am capable of deciding for myself what direction I want to take, and I deserve to do so. This is my life, and I have the right to decide what's important to me. If I'm not exactly sure of what I want, I can make a list and make carefully thought-out choices for myself. I might find this difficult in the beginning, but with practice I will become more accustomed to planning my future and taking the path I've chosen.

➤ Day 271

Blame serves no purpose in my life. When I blame myself for past mistakes, it stops me from moving forward in a positive way. Feeling bad for what I once did or criticizing myself for not acting the way I think I should have doesn't help me grow or heal. Once I can admit to myself that I did the best I could at the time, I can move forward with the knowledge that my situation is different now. I can now make different and wiser choices, and I can stop blaming myself for what I did wrong in the past. The fact is that blaming myself causes me to spend too much time thinking about the past. The past is over and done with, and today is here. Today I will move forward in my life without blaming myself for what I can't change.

Today I can understand and accept that my children may have opinions of me that I don't like. My children might be at an age where they speak to me with disrespect or anger. I can accept that they're going through a challenging phase in their own lives and not take it personally. I can ask that they speak to me in a kind manner, no matter what their feelings. I can explain to them that I don't disagree with their feelings, but I do disagree with the way they're expressing them. I'm learning new ways of expressing myself, and my children can too. I might not always have their approval, but I don't have to change to accommodate them. I don't have to feel attacked by the way my children are speaking to me, but I can realize that they're expressing themselves in ways that need to change. I can help them learn how to talk in more appropriate ways without taking away from what they're trying to say. If they refuse to listen to me, I can always ask for help from a therapist or school counselor. Silence isn't always golden, but the tone of our voice can be.

➤ *Day 273*

How I choose to handle crisis today can be different from how I handled it in the past. Perhaps I used to panic while my heart rate went sky high, or I withdrew and ignored the intensity of the situation. Perhaps I struggled to breathe as I drowned in the turmoil. We teach young children to stop thrashing about in deep water and roll over on their backs and float instead. I can do the same in my times of crisis. I can stop panicking and fighting the situation and float through it instead. I can make decisions based on carefully thought-out plans and with consideration of the outcome. When I stop fighting and learn how to be at peace, I can genuinely say that I've effectively learned how to deal with crisis. Worrying and struggling won't change the outcome, and they can sometimes make it worse. Learning how to slow down while considering my options will help me get through a crisis more easily.

Interruptions can be frustrating, especially interruptions while I'm trying to speak. Do I find that others interrupt me when I'm trying to talk about something that's important to me? Do I then talk louder or begin to interrupt them in return? I have the right to say what I need to say without being interrupted, and others have the right to the same consideration. If I find myself in a conversation with someone who insists on interrupting me, I can ask that he or she let me finish first. In a planned confrontation, I can ask ahead of time that we take turns talking and not interrupt each other. Once the other person is finished, I can then repeat what I thought he or she said to make sure I understood it correctly. I can then take my turn to express my thoughts. Even in casual conversation, everyone deserves to talk without being interrupted. It takes practice, but I'm learning appropriate ways of expressing myself in a considerate, healthy manner, and I'm showing others how to do the same. Today, and from now on, I will not interrupt others while they're speaking.

Just as I discipline my children, I can learn self-discipline when necessary. Are there times when I should be acting more responsibly? Are there tasks that I should attend to but I'm ignoring by getting sidetracked or by stalling? If I think I need self-discipline, I can put myself on a schedule and stick to it. If I can't bring myself to complete a specific chore, I can schedule it during two-hour blocks of time. I will attend to the chore for two hours, then do something else. Perhaps I can go back to it again after thirty minutes for another two hours. Keeping myself responsible helps keep me independent, and it keeps me from needing to be rescued after I've created a mess of things. Today I can use discipline in my own life, which will help me learn how to be a more responsible adult.

➤ *Day 276*

Today I will be satisfied with what I have. Have I become so goal-oriented or focused on the future that I've forgotten to look at where I am? If I removed all the worries and concerns about tomorrow or next week, what do I have right now? If I took today and looked at it separately from any other day, what kind of day is it? I might find that what seems to be a bad day, looked at by itself, is a pretty good day. Today I will focus on the present and what I've accomplished in it. I will be satisfied and glad for what I have now, who I am now, and how far I've come. Being content and happy today puts me in a place of gratitude and appreciation, instead of feeling that I don't have enough. When I live my life as though I don't have enough or always need more, I will never be satisfied or happy. A large part of knowing how to live life without abuse is knowing and feeling comfortable with being happy.

Not everything is black and white, all or nothing, great or terrible. There are many parts of my life that can be gray areas, or just okay. When I notice these in-between areas, I don't have to struggle to change them. If I know something could be better and I know I can do something about it, then I can choose to meet the challenge. If I want to change a situation because it's just not good enough, but it seems nearly impossible to change, I can leave it alone at least for now. If one of my goals is to have a high-paying job that's satisfying, and I get a job that pays less than I wanted but is work that I love doing, I can let that be good enough. I can perceive my goal as being met because I found work that I love. Whatever my personal opinion is or however I view a situation, I can always remember that the middle of the road is okay and that gray areas do exist. Today I will remember that sometimes the middle is the best place to be.

I can be spontaneous without being careless. I might be hard on myself or feel pressure from others to be responsible, calculated, disciplined, timely, or serious. Even though those qualities are admirable and help me remain independent, I can still enjoy spontaneity. Today I will do one thing that is spontaneous. I will choose some kind of activity that wasn't in the plan for today, something that's not in my schedule, isn't expected, and doesn't take me away from necessary obligations. I will enjoy the activity simply because it is spontaneous, if for no other reason. Today I will learn what it means to keep a schedule *and* be spontaneous. Living my life in this way helps me to enjoy being both responsible and playful.

When I open my heart to others or share personal feelings with them, I might feel vulnerable. I might be afraid that they'll use the information to hurt me or that they'll leave me. When I risk sharing my feelings, I might feel fear but hide it behind anger. Do I find myself feeling angry or easily upset after I've shared personal feelings or allowed someone to get close to me? Am I angry because I'm beginning to care deeply about someone? Do I want to end a relationship because I don't want the other person to end it first? Today I will think about what it's like to feel vulnerable, and I'll make a list of the positive and negative outcomes of allowing it. On the negative side, I might write that if I'm vulnerable, I might lose a friend or lover. On the positive side, I might write that I will feel loved. When I'm done, I'll compare the two lists. Are my fears realistic? Have they happened before? What would I do if they came true? Today I will remind myself that if I stay out of relationships because of what *might* happen, I might miss out on some very satisfying friendships. After all, there are no guarantees in any relationship, and feeling vulnerable is a normal part of being human.

Who in my life will make me happy? Do I look to others when I'm feeling discouraged, sad, or lonely? Do I want someone to help me feel better? I hold within myself the ability to be happy. I don't have to put expectations on others to make me feel loved or special. I don't have to look for a new relationship to be happy; I can find it within me. When I try to be happy because of other people, it means they have the power to take my happiness away. When I make myself happy, I'm the one in control of my emotions. Today I will remember that I'm the one who's responsible for my happiness, not someone else. I don't have to look for someone else to fix my low self-esteem or attitude. Even though I can be upset by some people or feel happy when I'm with others, I'm the one who's creating these feelings because I have the ability to do so. The only person who *makes* me feel a certain way is me.

Today I will make time for my spiritual beliefs and allow myself to experience faith. I may have had trouble in the past with having faith, but there are some situations in which trusting is crucial. Even if I don't trust in myself or others, I can still trust my spiritual beliefs. I will begin by making positive statements in my prayers, acting as if I already have what I need. Rather than ask for patience, I can thank my Spiritual Power for the patience that I already have. When I pray for patience as if I don't have any, I'm sure to find myself in situations that try my patience. Likewise, if I pray for the ability to forgive others, I'm sure to find myself in situations where I need to practice forgiveness. If I give thanks for my ability to forgive, I acknowledge that I'm capable of forgiveness already. Today I will trust that my Spiritual Power gives me what I need at the exact time I need it. The truth is, my Spiritual Power has already provided me with what I need. I only have to recognize it.

Do I ever enjoy, even if only for a second, discovering that my problems are worse than someone else's? Do I participate in discussions about how badly I was abused to show that it was worse than someone else's past? Do I ever feel like I'm in competition with someone else for having the most abusive past? I don't have to do this. I can understand that any abusive past was a terrible experience and that all of us in abusive situations have something in common: we were hurt and didn't like it. Whenever I meet someone who was abused, or is being abused, I will look at her or him with compassion not competitiveness. We can support each other in our times of need. We can share how we felt about our experiences and how we feel about our challenges today. Competition and rivalry don't help me in my healing, but companionship and friendship do. Today I will reach out to others who have a similar background and not try to outdo them. Being hurt more than someone else doesn't make me special, but what I've learned from it and how much I've grown does.

Do I know how to receive? Do I feel guilty when I receive, believing deep inside that I don't deserve it? Do I know how to say thank you and show my appreciation, or does receiving oftentimes make me feel ashamed or embarrassed? Today, when someone gives me a gift or a compliment, I will believe that I deserve to be treated with kindness and say thank you. If I'm in need and someone offers me a loan, I will let go of feeling ashamed and say thank you for the offer. Even if I don't accept the offer, I can appreciate this person's care and desire to help. As long as I know that I'm not receiving because I've manipulated the situation in some way, I can receive with grace and dignity. As I become more self-reliant and independent, I will someday be able to help or give to others in the same way.

➤ *Day 284*

Today I will be aware of the different ways that people perceive situations. When I meet people who have never been exposed to abuse or abusive situations, it may be difficult for them to understand how I could have tolerated such behavior. They might not understand why I didn't leave. Their perspective is different from mine. When I meet someone who has a history of being abused, but whose healing process or decisions are different from mine, I will not judge her or him. That person's perspective is different from mine. If other people judge me too harshly because of where I am in my life, I will remember that their perspective is different from mine. I might believe that I've accomplished a lot, considering where I came from, but others might see me as having accomplished very little compared to where they think I should be. Everyone has a unique opinion and perspective on a situation. It's always important for me to consult with my therapist or support group to make sure I'm being realistic. But other than that, today I will accept that I don't have to please others. My perspective is the most important one for me to consider.

Today I will let go of procrastination. I will take a look at why I put off responsibilities and how I can change this behavior. Do I feel that I won't do certain tasks well enough or that they're too over-whelming? Do I set specific standards for myself and then fail because I've set them too high? Do I expect perfection from myself and then put off what I fear will be imperfect? As long as I accomplish my tasks to the best of my ability, I will succeed. I can jump in with both feet when necessary and feel proud that I at least started what I needed to do. Nothing can ever be completed without starting it first. When I procrastinate, I will never get where I need to go, and eventually I will become overwhelmed and buried underneath all the things I refused to start. Today I will let go of the desire to put off what needs to be done now.

Even though it has been quite some time since I was in an abusive relationship, do I still find myself feeling like a victim? Do I hold myself hostage because I feel pressured, ignored, or unjustly treated by others? Do I focus on what I don't have or become preoccupied with what I could have if life weren't so unfair? Today I will let go of my feelings of being mistreated and focus on being a winner. I *am* a winner because I was willing to leave abuse behind and stand up for myself. I might have become so accustomed to suffering that I don't know how to live without it. Today I will refuse to suffer anymore, and I'll focus on everything in my life that is good. I will not complain about injustice or unfairness for the next twenty-four hours. I will remember and acknowledge how much goodness there is around me, and I'll let go of feeling persecuted. Today I will see what I have instead of complaining about what I don't have.

Being persistent is different from being forceful. When I have to force something to happen or change, it's not something I really need. When I can meet my challenges and overcome obstacles by not giving up, I'm being persistent. When I'm persistent, I have the strength to accomplish what I set out to do, and I can be proud of my achievements. Today I will recognize when I'm being persistent and when I'm trying to force an issue. Force will feel different to me because I will probably hit a "brick wall" at every turn. This usually means that I need to change my direction and find other options. Persistently doing the footwork means I'm doing my part, but forcing things to be my way only shows that I'm unwilling to consider anything else. When I'm persistent, I have to keep trying, when it still feels like the right thing to do. Eventually I will be successful and rewarded in my efforts.

➤ Day 288

Do I handle my money responsibly? Do I spend too much money, saving nothing for a rainy day? Do I keep my purse strings so tight that I don't enjoy my life? Do I overcompensate for the times when I had nothing by spending too much money on things I don't need? Today I will take a look at my relationship with money. Has money become my new abuser? Do I feel mistreated or neglected because of money? I can make a list of ways I can change my relationship with money. Perhaps I need to change jobs or ask for a raise. Maybe I need to open a savings account or invest. I might even want to take a second job or start a home business. On the other hand, if I've been too stringent with my budget, I could withdraw a hundred dollars and go shopping. Whatever my challenges are with my money, I will look at how I relate to it and make changes where necessary.

Today I will recognize the object of my obsession. Is it cleaning my house? Is it my work or my hobby? Is it shopping? Is it food? Is it a person? What specific thing in my life is causing me to obsess? After I determine what it is, I will ask myself, what do I get by obsessing about this? What do I win, and what am I losing? Can I let go of focusing on this particular issue or object? If I were to stop obsessing, what would be left for me to do? Are there other responsibilities that need attention? Am I avoiding something of importance because of this obsession? Today, each time I begin to obsess, I will turn my attention to something else. I will create a diversion from my diversion. When I act obsessively, it prevents me from dealing with other issues in my life that require my attention too. I can read articles or books that talk about obsessive behavior and deal with it appropriately. Obsessing is a control issue, and I want to live without being controlled or having to be in control. I can learn how to live my life without being obsessive. I will give all the areas of my life the attention they require. I will learn how to stop using my obsession as a detour from what I need to be doing.

➤ *Day 290*

Today I will surrender to that which I cannot control. Surrender does not mean giving up when I need to be persistent; it means letting go of that which I can't change. Surrender doesn't mean I stop trying; it means I try, then I surrender to the outcome. If I need to find a place to live, I can look in the paper, on the Internet, in rental or real estate publications; I can ask friends or drive around and look. I can fill out applications, make a good impression, and follow up with phone calls. I can think positively by getting ready to move, asking friends to help, fixing up the place that I'm leaving, or imagining where I will put my furniture in a new place. But I will surrender to the outcome by not calling the landlord or real estate agent again and again. I will not repeatedly drive by the place where I hope to live or stop my search when I find a place I like. I will do my part and then surrender to the rest. I can believe and trust that whatever happens is for the best. What I think I want for myself—and what I may try to force—may not ultimately be in my best interest. I will let go of constantly thinking about and analyzing the situation, and I will surrender to whatever happens, no matter how long it takes.

➤ *Day 291*

Am I too quick to anger? Have I let frustration become a normal response to problems? Do I exhibit negativity most of the time? Have I come to expect that things will go wrong? When criticism and anger have become a way of life for me, it's time to change my attitude. For the next twenty-one days, every time something happens that would normally cause me to react negatively, I will say, "This is great!" It takes twenty-one days to change something that has become a habit. By changing my negative reaction to a positive one, I'm changing the way I view and respond to problems in my life. I can find the "silver lining" in every experience. If my children have misbehaved, I can recognize that even though they've done something wrong, I'm still grateful that they are in my life and are healthy. I can look at the positive side to everything that goes wrong, and I will challenge myself to find what it is. In any negative situation, I can make this statement and know that it will eventually give me a more positive outlook: This is great!

➤ *Day 292*

Do I feel the need to apologize whether or not something is my fault? In the past, I might have had to say I was sorry no matter who—if anyone—was to blame. Did my abuser blame me for things only to have an excuse to abuse me? Did he create problems so he could then blame me? Did I feel the need to constantly take responsibility for everything that had gone wrong, or anything he was accusing me of, even if I had nothing to do with it? Today I will examine when and why I apologize. When I say I'm sorry, is there really something that I've done wrong? Did I really make a mistake, or am I just trying to fix a situation by assuming the responsibility? I don't have to say I'm sorry or apologize for anything that I didn't cause or create. There's a big difference between being sorry and feeling sorry that something has happened. If a close friend has a problem or is experiencing a difficult situation, I can say that I'm sorry about it. But I didn't cause it, and I probably can't fix it. Being compassionate doesn't mean I shoulder the blame for the problems of others; it means I can openly care about what happens to people who are important to me.

I don't have to apologize when I set boundaries for myself that don't meet the approval of others. When I'm clear about what I want and what is okay in my life, I can clearly express it to others. If they don't like it or it doesn't fit into what they want, I can accept that we don't agree and that we have different needs. I don't have to say I'm sorry for not being like them or for making decisions that don't please them. I can be sorry that we don't agree, but I don't have to be sorry that I've set boundaries for myself. I have the right and I deserve to make the choices in my life that I feel are best for me. Today I will understand that I don't have to say I'm sorry when my decisions don't make other people happy.

Do I feel that others respect me? Do I think my children respect me? Do I provide a good role model for them? Do I speak to them in a respectful tone of voice and without blame or guilt? When I speak to others in ways that show respect and in a tone of voice that is appropriate, I will usually get back what I give. It's also important to know, when trying this method of communication, that it will take time for others to change how they've been talking to me. If I begin speaking to my children in new ways, I can't expect that they will immediately respond. If, for their entire lives, I've been yelling and arguing with them, I can expect some resistance and reluctance to change now, when I try to sit and have a calm discussion with them. If I make a positive change in the way I speak to those around me, and if I'm persistent in healthy communication, others will eventually begin to relate to me in similar ways. I might have to let others know that I'm trying to change the way I talk to them and ask them to practice along with me. By practicing the way we talk and act toward each other, we are all growing and becoming more effective in our relationships.

Often, the people who are close to me share similar ways of thinking, acting, or spending time. This doesn't mean that we have to share everything. We can choose which activities we do together and allow each other to have separate interests too. If I'm in an intimate relationship, but want to go to a movie with friends, it should be perfectly acceptable. It doesn't mean there are problems in my relationship, but that the relationship is healthy and equal. Problems would exist when one person wants to have the freedom to choose separate activities but doesn't allow the other the same consideration. It is normal and healthy to have experiences, hobbies, and interests that are separate from those of my children, friends, or romantic interest. Couples and families shouldn't be expected to enjoy everything together. If someone I care about has told me he or she wants to do something away from me, I can react by saying, "This is great!" Today I will understand that this doesn't mean the person no longer loves me or is losing interest. It means that person is emotionally healthy enough to have his or her own interests and respects me enough to allow me mine.

Today I will review my goals and determine whether they're realistic. Have I set goals for myself that will ultimately set me up for failure? Have I become so accustomed to falling short of my goals that I just assume I'll never make it? I can look at my goals and decide whether they're within my capabilities, and if they're not, I will change them. Is one of my goals to live in a mansion or make an unrealistic amount of money? Do I want to drive a sports car that I would never be able to afford? I can revise my goals to fit what I believe I can achieve. It's okay for me to set goals that are a little higher than where I am today, but if I set my goals too high, I might feel defeated before I even begin. Goals are different than dreams. I can have a separate list of dreams for myself, where all my outrageous desires can be kept. I can review them occasionally and find pleasure in seeing myself living my dreams. It is equally important, if not more, to set realistic goals that I can achieve within the near future. I need to learn how it feels to complete something worthwhile and be able to say each step of the way, "This is great!"

Real life is not always about sharing intimate and private information. I may have discovered in my support group, or with my therapist, that sharing in this manner was necessary for my healing. I don't need to open myself up completely in all my relationships, however. I can keep some things private. If I begin a new romantic relationship, I can choose what I share and what I don't. I don't have to divulge my entire past or every step of my progress. I can discuss past feelings or experiences and at the same time be vague about the details. Perhaps I want someone to know that loud noises scare me or that yelling makes me sick to my stomach. I can do this without revealing the details of past incidents. I can simply say that because of past relationships, these things upset me. People who truly care about me will listen to me and respect my feelings. If they want to know more, I can tell them that I don't want to go into it or that I don't feel comfortable discussing it. I can choose what I explain and what I don't. I can ask that others respect my privacy.

Today I will look at my past and find those things for which I can be grateful. I don't have to be grateful for being hit, hurt, abused, degraded, or abandoned. I can be grateful for what I learned from it. Perhaps I learned to be cautious or careful. I might have learned how to recognize what I don't want in relationships. I might have learned how to stand up for myself and when to say stop. I might have come away from my past with a better appreciation of my children or how to best show them I love them. I've learned how to set goals for myself, how to deal with worries or obsessions, and how to make decisions on my own. What about my past has served me well in my new life? Have I become a more understanding person because of where I've been? Am I more able to recognize a loving person when I see one? Can I recognize and appreciate honesty or the fact that I no longer have to make excuses? Am I able to be a better friend, mother, or father because of the lessons in my past? Today I will take the good out of the bad and keep it. I can throw out all the terrible and frightening memories and hold on to what I can appreciate.

Abuse can cover a wide range of behaviors, from criticism to severe or fatal battering. Oftentimes people believe that if they don't have bruises or broken bones, their relationship isn't abusive. They don't realize that words can hurt more than fists. Criticizing others, withholding feelings, not setting boundaries and then becoming angry, refusing to talk, calling people names, playing mind games, or humiliating others are all forms of abuse without physical force. These types of abuse are so subtle that many people don't even realize they're being abused. Today I will recognize these behaviors as being abusive. Just because someone isn't hitting me doesn't mean we have a good relationship. I will not tolerate any form of abuse in my life, from anyone. I will seek out people who are capable of healthy communication, love and affection, handling their anger appropriately, and expressing themselves with honesty and integrity. I deserve to have these types of people in my life, and I will not settle for less.

If I find that I'm in another abusive relationship, I know now that I don't have to try to make it work. I can get out of the relationship before it gets worse and before I'm in too deep. I don't have the time, or the desire, to stay in another abusive situation. I've come too far since the last one. I might be tempted to make excuses such as "this time it's different," or "it's not as bad as before," or "he loves me more than the last one did," or "he's so good with the kids," or "he said it'll get better," or "he didn't really mean to yell at me," or . . . or . . . or . . . The face may be different, but the end result will be the same, if not worse. Abuse is progressive. If it doesn't seem that bad, I can be sure it'll get worse. Today I will remind myself that my worst day of being alone is better than my best day of being abused. I deserve better, and I will have it. I will find the courage, once again, to get out of relationships that are abusive in any way, shape, or form. I'm not a failure for choosing another abuser; I'm successful for recognizing it and getting out.

➤ *Day 301*

There are important steps I need to take if I want new relationships to last. I need to allow a new relationship to grow in a healthy way by giving it the time it needs. When I go too fast in a relationship, necessary stages are overlooked, and I might find myself in a relationship destined to fail. When trees are planted and their roots aren't given enough time to grow deeply into the soil, they're sure to fall during a storm. When the roots are given time to grow slowly, strongly, and deeply, they will most likely weather any storm. Relationships can be similar, because when they're taken too quickly, they're likely to fail at the first sign of difficulty. But if given the time to grow, they will withstand the winds of turmoil and crisis. If I meet someone I want to be with, I can care for our relationship by not going too fast. I will remind myself that a tree needs tender care and nurturing to grow and flourish, not fertilizers and chemicals that force it to grow faster. Today I will take care of my new relationship by understanding what it takes to make it strong and lasting.

Today I will make a list of romantic relationships that didn't last. I will first write the list without stopping to think about the past; I will simply write names. Perhaps there are many names, perhaps just a few or only one. After my list is complete, I will make a quick note by each name about why I feel the relationship didn't last. I don't have to write pages of explanations, just a few words. When I'm finished, I will review these notes. Are there any similarities? Do I see any patterns? Do I blame the problems on others, or do I take responsibility for my part? Were they all abusive? Were they progressively abusive, meaning that my first relationships might not have been so difficult, but as time went on they became more dangerous or harmful? When I read my list, I will identify the reasons that seem to have repeated themselves and write them on the side. This exercise helps me to better see the patterns in my past relationships so that I might recognize them sooner in future relationships. I'm learning more about myself and my past each day. Everything I do has a purpose, and the purpose ultimately is to keep myself safe and alive.

Today I will add to yesterday's list the names of friends and family members whose relationships have not been fulfilling for me. If I've had friends who moved away or family members who are no longer living, I don't have to include them on my list. The people I need to add are those with whom I've had problems or disputes that affected our relationships. I will write short notes or a few words next to each name regarding why our relationship ended or changed. As before, I will review the list to find similarities. Did I have friends or family members who were abusive to me? Did I cause any of the problems? Did I choose friends who didn't deserve my trust? Did my friends use or manipulate me? This exercise is continuing to help me recognize problem areas in my past relationships. It helps me recognize what didn't work in the past, so that friendships now can be more satisfying and genuine. Abuse doesn't happen only with romantic partners. It can happen with friends and family too. Today I'm continuing on my path of self-discovery to ensure that relationships in all areas of my life are giving, loving, healthy, and equal.

Today I will complete the last part of the exercise with my relationship list. I will look at my notes on both lists and compare them. Do I find the same problems in all my relationships? What might I have done to avoid these problems? Were there warning signs that I saw early on and chose to ignore? Were my feelings in the relationships similar to each other? Today I will write what I would like to say to all the people on my list. I can ask questions such as "Why did you hurt me like that?" or "Wasn't I a good friend to you?" I can also make statements such as "I never should have trusted you" or "I hate what you did to me!" When I'm finished, I will read each statement out loud. If this exercise is too difficult for me, I can choose to discuss it with my therapist, sponsor, or support group. Recovering from abuse may be difficult, but learning how to move on and fly free can be even more challenging. I'm up to it, and I'm determined to spread my wings.

➤ *Day 305*

Today I will accept the fact that things might not always look positive on the outside. When young children are learning how to walk, it's a miraculous sight. They're so full of energy as they clumsily lift each foot, laughing all the while, and during this momentous display, they usually fall. Does that discourage them? Do they stop trying? Do they complain that this wasn't in their plans? Do they sit and contemplate why this is happening to them? No. Like these children, I will pick myself up after a fall, realizing it's all part of the process. Learning new things isn't always easy, doesn't always look pretty, and doesn't always feel great. But just like the young child, with enough time and practice, I will eventually be running with the confidence of a champion. Today I will remind myself that after 305 days, I am a champion.

What do I wish for? Do I wish that someday my life will be easier? Do I wish to find a better job? Do I wish for a raise in pay? Do I wish that my children would be more respectful? Do I wish that someday I'll meet someone who loves me the way I want to be loved? Do I wish my abuser would never bother me again? Today I will buy a bottle of bubbles. I will go to a park, a river, a lake, my backyard, or some other place out in the open. I will take out the wand and blow the bubbles into the wind. As I watch them blow away, I will imagine that each bubble holds one of my wishes. In my mind, I am blowing my wishes into the bubbles and letting them fly into the world. I will imagine that as I watch them, they're coming true in their own time. I can let go of trying to control the bubbles and be glad that I feel free enough to even have wishes. In the past, I probably had just one wish: that things could be different. Now I have many wishes, and I find pleasure in knowing that the old wish from long ago came true.

Today I will compare my life to how it was before. As I look around, what do I notice? Are my surroundings different? In what way? What did I give up to have what I have now? When I first left my abuser, I probably didn't have any idea of what my life would be like. When I let go of being abused and feeling the need to help someone who was beyond help, I opened a new door. What came through the door? Do I now have peace of mind? Do I have the freedom to choose my own friends? Do I now plan my own day? Do I now have the freedom to watch the TV shows I want to watch? Am I now able to walk in the door without being afraid of someone else's mood? How does my life now compare to my life in the past? I will make a list of everything I have now that I didn't have before, materially and emotionally. I can allow myself to feel grateful, and I can appreciate the changes. I will keep my list, and each day I will add things to it. This will help me realize how much I've gained and how much I've received. Sometimes the best way to clearly see how much I have is to remember how much I didn't have in the past.

➤ Day 308

I've learned about not giving up my own needs for the sake of pleasing others, and what it means to be codependent. I've probably, in an effort to change, behaved in ways that others perceived as selfish. When I'm taking care of myself and what I need, I'm not being selfish. Today I understand that recovery from codependency is essential in my healing, but so is being emotionally available to my children. I shouldn't ignore my needs, but sometimes I might need to put them on hold. I will be there when my children need me, whether it's because they have a problem, they need special time with me, or I need to spend more than a few minutes tucking them in at night. When I'm emotionally available to my children, I show them that they matter, that they're special, that I love them, and that they deserve to be loved. They have been through a rough time right along with me, and it's absolutely necessary that I show them how much they mean to me. I'm not being codependent if I spend time taking care of or just being with my children.

If I meet someone who is in an abusive situation, I will not become overly involved. There are five simple things I can say to help a battered person:

1. I'm afraid for your safety.
2. I'm afraid for the safety of your children.
3. It's only going to get worse.
4. You don't deserve to be treated that way.
5. I have a phone number you can call when you're ready to talk about this problem (have the local or national hot line number ready).

Any of these statements help me to stay detached, but also help the other person to realize that the situation is serious. I can make the choice to stay uninvolved by giving out a phone number for professionals who can help instead of my own phone number. I need to realize that this person is in crisis. Are my children and I ready to take on another person's crisis? I'm not being coldhearted, callous, or selfish if I choose to stay detached. There are many agencies, shelters, and advocates that will help a woman leave. I don't have to be the one to save her.

Many people, even after all the media coverage and discussion of domestic violence, still don't understand it. They don't know why women stay or how they could even have become involved in the first place. They don't know about the dynamics of an abusive relationship. They might still believe that women "drive" their abusers to violence. They might agree that although there are men who are certainly capable of violence, it's the woman's fault for not seeing it before becoming involved with them. Let's get real. Women do not cause abusers to be violent. Abusers are abusive because they learned, somewhere, that it's an answer to their frustration, a response to feeling out of control. Usually, it has become habitual. Normal, loving, nurtured children don't grow up and suddenly decide to become abusive. Something along the way taught them to do so. Children also don't plan to grow up and marry an abuser. Something along the way causes them to misunderstand what love feels like. Today I accept that not everyone is going to understand what happened to me. What matters is that I'm learning how to understand it.

Today I will take responsibility for the reasons I chose to stay. First, I will make a list of the things I told myself when I thought about leaving. Did I believe that I had to keep the family together at all costs? Did I feel that I would betray my religious beliefs? Was I afraid that I couldn't make it on my own? Was I too ashamed to admit what was happening? Was I afraid that no one else would want me? Was I afraid my abuser would kill me, or himself, or the children? Did I believe that things would change? Did I think that if I hung in there long enough, I could save him and stop the abuse? Did I feel sorry for that poor little boy, all grown up now, who'd had such a terrible childhood? Once I've completed my list, I will accept that, at the time, no one could have convinced me these things weren't true. As I look at my list, I won't be too hard on myself. I won't criticize myself for having the beliefs that I did. Today I will admit that I had my reasons for not leaving, and, at the time, I thought they were good ones. I will never allow myself to be abused again, no matter what reason I'm given.

Today I will loosen up. Have I become rigid in my thinking? Are my household rules too strict? Do I become frantic when things don't happen the way I think they should? Do I keep myself or my children on a strict daily routine? I will review the way I run my home and determine if I need to be more lenient. Are there areas of my life in which I can relax a little? Can I change some of the rules? Am I willing to let go of my attachment to having things be perfect? Am I compulsive about things such as housecleaning, work, or schedules? Today I will review my life and let go of that which serves no other purpose than to give me complete control. Does it really matter, if I'm having a good time with my children, that the house gets messy? Does it really matter if they get to bed thirty minutes late because we were watching a movie together? Would anyone really be hurt if the dishes didn't get done tonight? I will continue to practice letting go as I embrace spontaneity. I will practice being more flexible and begin to include the words *leave it until later* in my vocabulary. Balance, balance is the key.

➤ *Day 313*

Just as domestic violence and abusive behavior are progressive, so is my healing. Each day I get stronger, more aware, more courageous, more decisive, more independent, and more alive. I can feel myself moving in directions I never thought I would. I'm a great person, a fantastic learner, and a willing participant in my own life. I've accomplished great feats of bravery, and I deserve a pat on the back, a trophy, an award, a blue ribbon, a medal! Today I will be proud of myself. I'm a survivor, a good example, a success story, and one of the most magnificent people I know. Today I will give myself a present. It might be that new dress, a new pair of shoes, a box of chocolates, a card, or a movie I've been wanting to see. Whatever I decide to give myself, I will realize I am worth it.

Today I will remind myself that when someone is interested in me, I must be accepted as a package deal. If someone likes me because I'm attractive, funny, generous, or kind, he or she should also accept all the other parts of me. I have many qualities and emotions, feelings and ideas, morals and habits. I'm an entire package and not willing to give up any part of myself in order to please someone else. A true friend, lover, or partner is someone who is willing to accept the whole me. I can't truly feel loved if only one part of me is loved. I must be appreciated for all that I am: good or bad, positive or negative, afraid or courageous. I admit that there are things I need to change for the better, and I'm willing to work on them. But for now, I deserve to be loved for all that I am, not all that I will be. I deserve to have the people close to me accept everything about me.

When someone wants to become involved in my life, he or she should know that my children are part of the package too. Should I decide that my relationship with this person has some kind of future, I will consider how this person interacts with my children. Is this someone whom my children will like? Will they respect this person? Will they be afraid of this person or feel safe with him? Will they have fun together? Will they be able to communicate? These are just some of the questions I will ask when choosing new relationships. My children have probably had their share of bad examples of role models. I must make sure that anyone new in my life is going to show them how things can be different. I want to show my children that there are people we can trust, with whom we can feel safe. I want to show my children that they deserve to be loved just as much as I do. Not only am I a package deal in myself, but my children are part of the package too.

➤ Day 316

Today I will learn about negotiation. Negotiation is when two people work to come up with a plan or agreement that is beneficial to both of them: a win-win situation. Negotiation can take place when accepting a job, buying a car, dealing with children, or confronting another adult. I deserve to participate in win-win situations, but I can't negotiate for something if I don't know what I want. In the past, I might have settled for whatever decisions were made by my abuser. I don't have to do that anymore. I don't have to settle for the first offer. Once I get a picture in my mind of what I want, I can negotiate for it. If someone offers me a job, I don't have to accept the salary or pay that is initially offered. I can ask to have added responsibility in order to receive higher pay. This lets a prospective employer know that I would like more money, but I'm willing to work for it. I don't have to accept the deal that a car dealer initially offers. Even if I have poor credit history, I can negotiate for a better deal. If my counteroffer is rejected, I can practice acceptance or be willing to walk away. Today I will read a book, look on the Internet, buy a tape, or go to the library to learn what I can about negotiation.

I can take care of myself when I'm in pain. If I'm having painful thoughts or feelings, I will realize that I have within myself tools that will bring me comfort. I can write a letter, talk to my therapist, pray, make a list, make a worry wall, put notes in my God box or goal box, talk to a friend, call a hot line, go to a support group, or write in my journal. I have many tools available to me, and I know how to use them. These tools help me to process information and move through a problem that might have stopped me in my tracks before. I may have reacted to problems in the past by becoming emotionally paralyzed and afraid to do anything. Today I will use the tools that I have at my disposal and be grateful for them. Problems that used to stop me like brick walls may now seem like stepping stones. I'm grateful for all the tools that I have now and for the willingness to handle my problems as they come, without having to look to someone else to fix them.

When I say no, I will mean no. Many people try to be nice when rejecting an idea or suggestion. They might try to let the other person down easy or explain why they're opposed. I don't have to explain why I don't agree with or don't want to do something. I just need to say no. I don't have to say "maybe" or "I'll think about it" or "maybe another time" when what I really mean is no. I have the right to say no without explanation. My children have probably become accustomed to asking why, and it might have become habit for me to explain. I might feel the need to explain why to anyone who asks me. Having had a past where explanations were commonplace, I now realize that I don't have to explain myself, and especially not when I'm saying no. No simply means no. If I find myself saying no when I really mean "I might change my mind later," then I can say what I mean. When I want the chance to think about it, or to make a decision later, I can say so. Today I will practice saying no when I really mean no.

I like feeling connected with others. I like the feeling of belonging and being able to trust someone. I cherish companionship, friendship, and intimacy. I like these feelings, even though my experiences with them may have been hurtful or even dangerous. In my new life without abuse, I might be afraid to make new friends or let someone get close to me. This is normal, given that I was mistreated or betrayed by someone I loved. In time, it is important for me to learn how to trust again and allow myself to open up to other people. At the same time, it is more important for me to watch for red flags, set boundaries, express myself using effective communication, and know how to say no. Once I've learned about these skills, I will practice using them. In order for me to feel connected to others, I need to establish ground rules—boundaries—and take relationships slowly as I determine whether they are safe. I enjoy feeling connected with others, but not at a great expense. I will be willing to get close to other people while using the tools that I've acquired in the last few months.

I like to feel good about myself, and I feel good about myself when I know that others appreciate me. It's normal for me to enjoy being needed and to feel good when others approve of me. As long as I'm respecting my own boundaries, living according to my own goals, and not giving up my own needs, it is perfectly okay to like it when others approve of me. What is most important is that I approve of me, but when others do, too, it makes me feel even better. Everyone likes to feel that they're doing well or are good at something. Everyone likes to hear that they are doing a good job, have special talents, or are contributing something of value. As long as I know I'm following my path, I can enjoy it when others notice it too.

➤ *Day 321*

Some potentially dangerous people will attempt to get close to me by using statements that cause me to feel guilty or bad about myself. If a person on the street asks for money, and I refuse or continue walking, he or she might say, "You think you're too good for me?" or something similar. These statements are meant to hook me into conversation, and I don't have to respond. If I were to turn around and defend myself or make excuses for why I didn't give the person money, I've fallen into his or her trap. The best thing I can do for myself is to say nothing. Because I'm used to having to explain myself or my actions, I might feel that I need to do so in this type of situation, but I don't. I don't have to explain to anyone, much less a stranger, why I'm behaving a certain way. To do and say nothing may seem cold or callous, but I'm keeping myself safe, and that is my highest priority. Today I don't have to defend or explain myself to anyone. I don't have to speak to people I don't know, whether at my apartment building, on public transportation, or in any public setting. I will keep myself safe, and this means not engaging in conversation with people who might pose a threat to me or my family.

➤ *Day 322*

In the past, I probably had developed a strong ability, and a strong need, to rationalize my situation. I might have had to make excuses for why my abuser acted as he did. I might have told myself that he didn't mean to do it, he couldn't help it, or it was my fault. Today I will pay attention to when I'm rationalizing current situations and bring myself back to reality. I will pay attention to how I really feel and stop trying to find a reason for the situation. If I experience apprehension or a gut feeling that something is wrong, I will not make an excuse for it. A red flag is actually my intuition telling me that something isn't right. I don't have to explain it away or ignore it; I need to listen to it and value it. If I meet someone who seems to be nice, but I still feel uneasy, I need to honor that feeling. I don't have to confront the person, talk about my feelings, or make an accusation. I just need to listen to that little voice and act accordingly. I'm not being silly, overly sensitive, crazy, or paranoid if I sense danger. My gut feelings will serve me well if I pay attention to them.

No one likes to be humiliated or embarrassed. I've experienced my share of these feelings in the past, and I didn't like it then, nor do I like it now. The key to handling these emotions is to first decide why I'm feeling embarrassed. Is it because of some belief that I have about myself? Is it low self-esteem or insecurity? Is someone else trying to embarrass me? If I experience embarrassment, I will look at why. If it is because of my own insecurities, and no one is trying to make me feel this way, then I have to deal with it myself. If possible, I can ask whoever has embarrassed me to stop their behavior, letting them know that it's hurting my feelings. Sometimes people make inappropriate jokes and don't realize that someone else in the group might be sensitive to their comments. If someone is trying to hurt me, I can ask that person to stop. If he or she refuses to do so, I can leave, express my anger, or, if I'm feeling emotionally strong enough, ignore her or him. I will not allow other people to purposely humiliate me or embarrass me for the sake of their own pleasure. I'm not a victim anymore, nor will I behave like one.

➤ *Day 324*

When I meet new people, I will not only focus on their good qualities but will also be aware of traits that are undesirable or possibly dangerous. I have the right to ask others what they do when they become angry. I might also ask how they feel about domestic violence. I would be interested to know if they think that women drive men to become violent. I could ask if they think some women deserve to be hit. Noticing how someone behaves in calm situations is one thing, because in the beginning, most batterers will be nice and charming. Even if I don't see any signs of rage or violent behavior, I can still ask what they think about certain situations such as Nicole Brown Simpson's murder. This is sure to initiate some kind of discussion in which I'll be able to see their point of view. Nonviolent, healthy people won't react to these types of questions in anger or with excuses for their beliefs. Often, people do who have something to hide. I'm done with people who have something to hide. I want to have relationships with people who believe that domestic violence is not an option.

When I let myself get overwhelmed with "what if" questions, I'm not able to see clearly what is happening right now. While it's important to plan and be prepared, I will not let myself become detached from what is happening around me. If I'm afraid of everything, consumed by all the bad things that could happen to me, I'm no longer using the intuitive abilities that can keep me safe. If I'm afraid of every situation, every stranger, every new encounter, every person I meet, then my ability to notice the things that might be dangerous or harmful to me becomes weak. I will pay attention to the things around me that actually warrant my being afraid. A dark figure following me down the street at night is frightening. Death threats from my abuser should scare me. On the other hand, a stranger playing with his dog at the park, in the daytime, probably isn't a threat to me. If I live in fear all the time, how can the most dangerous situations stand out? Today I will let go of "what ifs" and pay attention to what is going on right now. When I focus on what *might* happen, I might not notice what *is* happening.

Today I will make a commitment to be genuine. I will make a promise to myself to be who I really am, completely. I will be as honest and real as I can be, showing my true qualities. I no longer have to hide my feelings, emotions, or thoughts. I can be exactly who I am without shame, without embarrassment, without guilt, and without fear. I can show the real me, not the one I think people will like. I will not give false compliments or encouragement. When I like something or someone, I will tell the truth. I don't have to hide my beliefs. I can choose whom I share personal feelings with and stay true to myself. I will not play mind games with others or with myself. I can be exactly who I am, right now, and love myself for it. I'm happy with who I am becoming. I'm glad for the growth I've experienced, the skills I've developed, and the knowledge I've acquired. My life has not always been easy, but I am finding that being myself has become easier than I thought possible. In the past, I might not even have known where my abuser ended and I began, because our lives were so enmeshed in each other. But today I'm independent and separate from anyone else, and I like who I am.

Today I will look at the things in my life that make sense. In the past, there were many things that didn't make sense, and I either created reasons that helped me make sense of them or lived in confusion. Today I can look around at what does make sense. Getting up and going to work makes sense. I need to have an income, and going to work provides me with that. When I'm lonely and I feel sad, that makes sense. Sadness is a normal response to feeling lonely. When I'm tired, I go to sleep. No one forces me to stay up and listen to endless rages or accusations. Listening to my body and what it needs makes sense. When something good happens, I feel happy, and that makes sense. There's no one around to scream at me or hit me, ruining my good mood. Sometimes things happen that don't make sense, such as tragedies I see on the news or read about in the newspaper, but I can be aware of the things in my life that do make sense. I can be happy for the progress in my life and all that I've accomplished. Leaving my abuser made sense. Living without abuse makes sense. My feelings and emotions might not always make sense, but the fact that I'm able to have them does.

Today I will be awesome. In whatever I choose to do, I will be awesome in my efforts. I will not do something halfway or without commitment. I will be totally committed to whatever task I attempt, and I will allow myself the chance to surpass what I thought I could do. I will do an awesome job, because I'm an awesome person. I believe, in spite of whatever anyone else thinks, that I can achieve what I set out to accomplish. I can not only accomplish it but can also do an outstanding job. Today is an awesome day, and I will choose to live it that way.

Today I will let go of unnecessary baggage. Anything that I've been holding on to that is no longer of use to me, whether it's material or emotional, I will let go of now. Maybe it's time to clean out that closet or get rid of those old letters. Maybe I need to write letters to people with whom I need closure. Perhaps I need to let go of feeling defeated and start looking at how I've won. Today I will take all the things in my life that no longer have a positive purpose and throw them out. A good rule would be that if I haven't needed an object in a year, I can get rid of it. I can throw it out, give it away, sell it, or burn it. However I dispose of these unnecessary things, I will get rid of them now.

Today I will look at the caring side of me. Do I still care about things that aren't important anymore? Do I care about people who once hurt me? Do I wish I cared more about my responsibilities? Do I wish my capacity for caring would increase? Do I care too much? Today I will put more perspective on how much, or how little, I care about situations and people in my life. If I need to show that I care about my children a little more, I will tell them I love them twice a day, for no apparent reason. If I feel that's difficult for me to remember, I will say it before each meal. If I create a schedule for myself when dealing with things that are new or foreign, they will eventually become easier and part of my routine. If I find that I care about others too much, I will refrain from making controlling statements. I will allow others to live their lives without my constant expressions of concern. Too much caring is a form of control. I no longer wish to live in a controlled environment, even if the person causing it is me.

➤ *Day 331*

Today I will look at the drama in my life. Even though I'm not with an abuser anymore, how much drama is left in my life? Do I create drama by overreacting, by controlling, or by being insecure? Drama no longer serves a purpose in my life, and I will avoid it when possible. I don't have to create a crisis or dramatic situation in order to feel something. In the past, I might not have felt that I had any feelings at all during the times that were calm or peaceful. I will realize that I *do* have feelings when things are quiet; I just need to recognize them. I don't have to be upset or angry to feel alive. I'm just as alive when I'm reading, talking quietly, resting, cooking dinner, or engaged in any other activity that isn't noisy or out of control. Today I will let go of drama or crisis and no longer instigate them in my life. I will be aware of my feelings during the quiet times.

How much enthusiasm do I have? Am I motivated to meet my goals? Do I look forward to going to work? Do I get excited about preparing meals? Today I will look at the silver lining in everything I do. When I dread cooking, I will appreciate that there's food in the house. If I'm angry at my children, I will appreciate that they're safe. If I'm depressed about going to work, I will be glad for my paycheck, which enables me to live without assistance from others. When I look beyond disappointment or tasks that I find unpleasant, I will always find something in them to ignite my enthusiasm. I can change my attitude about them by looking for the positive or making them fun. How would I feel about work if I wore cartoon boxer shorts under my suit? Would my day be any different if I took a new way home? Would housecleaning be more productive if we set a timer and tried to "beat the clock"? Today I will find a way to be enthusiastic about the parts of my life that aren't always fun or pleasant. When I can find something positive in ordinary events, I'll be making my life more positive all the way around.

If I could choose my own fortune, what would it be? If I could write my own fortune cookie, what would it say? If I were my own palm reader, what would I see? Would my fortunes be warnings or fear-provoking statements? Would I say that the best is yet to be, that I should keep my chin up and think positively? Somewhere there has to be a happy medium. I can be cautious and feel optimistic at the same time. I don't have to ignore one to have the other. It is possible that my outlook, my way of living, my choices, and my decisions *do* affect my fortune. Why wait and hope for someone else to tell me about my destiny when the best person to do it is me? I don't have to go through one hundred fortune cookies hoping for a fortune I like; I can begin today by writing my own. Today I will write down my fortune: "She who lives her life without violence will . . ." or "He who lives his life without violence will . . ." With so much knowledge and support, with all the tools I've been given, I'm perfectly capable of predicting my future, knowing where I want to go.

Today I will choose my heroes. Heroes are people who have shown great courage and strength, and who are noted for their special achievements. Of all the people I've known, heard about, or read about, who are my heroes? Do I have a hero? Have I ever really thought about it? Today I will research the people I think I might admire or, if I already know who they are, I will write about why I consider them heroes. What qualities do they possess? What about them attracts me to them? Why do I think they're special? Do they have qualities that I would like to have? Are there any similarities between them and me? I can include my children in this exercise by asking them who their heroes are. This will give me a better idea of their values and ideals, as they get a better idea of mine. Today is about heroes, what being a hero means, who heroes are, and why we admire them. When I do this exercise, I learn more about myself, my values, and what's important to me.

➤ *Day 335*

Today is about joy. I can think about the difference between the things that brought me joy while I was being abused and the things that bring me joy today. In the past, I might have felt joy in the absence of screaming or violence. I might have found joy in fantasizing about a different life, a pleasant memory, or a friendly face, or I might have sought joy in my hope that things would soon be different. Today I may find joy in waking up to a quiet house, in my freedom, in the kind words of my children, or in the gift of a true friend. Today, as I look at the differences between the two lifestyles, I will be aware of how much of my time is joyful now compared with before. Today I will find joy in the fact that my life is better and in the hopes and dreams that I have for my future.

Knowledge is information that we are aware of, familiar with, or understand based on experience or studies. Today I will consider how much knowledge I've gained through experience, whether experiences of my own or those of others. I'm so much more aware than I was when I first said about my abuser, "If only I had known." No matter what kind of formal education I have, how far I went in school, or what kinds of grades I received, I now have a significant amount of knowledge about domestic violence. I've acquired enough knowledge to last a lifetime, and, fortunately for me, that's what I have now: a lifetime.

It takes a stronger person to lead than it does to control. People who control others don't care about what others want or need. They make rules based on what *they* think is best or what *they* want. A leader is someone who takes everyone's best interest to heart, makes appropriate decisions, encourages others, and promotes teamwork. Today I will determine whether I'm a leader or a controller. When I interact with my children or co-workers, do I promote a sense of teamwork? Does my behavior encourage others to do their best, or do they feel resentful toward me? Do I feel that my way is the only way and refuse to listen to the opinions of others? In the past, I didn't like it when my abuser made all the rules. I no longer want to have situations in my life where one person makes all the decisions and has all the control, even if that person is me. Even though I'm ultimately responsible for making decisions concerning my children, I can still listen to their viewpoints and feelings. When I make calculated, informed decisions, others will respect me for my wisdom. I want to be a leader whom others follow out of respect, not fear.

Today I will be a magnet for all things that are good for me. I will attract friends I can trust, material possessions that I want or need, and positive relationships. In the past, I might have felt that I was a magnet for things that were bad for me. I might have said to myself, "Why do I always end up with losers?" or "Why can't I meet someone who's good to me?" When I have low self-esteem and don't really believe that I deserve anything good, I will attract things that aren't good for me. It is with this attitude that I attract negative people who use or abuse me. This doesn't mean that being abused was my fault. It means that I was probably more open to accepting less than I deserved, or I settled for less than I wanted. Today I will be a magnet for love and happiness. I can imagine that good things are coming my way, that they're all around me and are waiting for me to accept them. I will say to myself, "I'm a magnet for good things in my life. I'm now open and willing to having everything that I want." Even if I might not believe it fully now, if I keep saying it to myself, I'll eventually change my mind and the things I attract.

➤ Day 339

If my life were like a ship on the sea, today I will be the navigator. I may have been used to someone else steering my ship or telling me which way to go. I may have felt that I had no control over my own life, and I probably didn't. Today I will mentally throw overboard those who would harm me. I will take the wheel and read my own map. I will decide which way my ship will go and which route I will take. Even though I may choose to have a crew of advisers who can help me, I will be the one to chart my course. I will realize that on the sea of life, I can't control the weather, but I'm perfectly capable of adjusting my sails.

➤ *Day 340*

Today I'm open to new ways of thinking. In my abusive relationship, there was often only one way to think: the way of my abuser. The way I saw things, and even the thoughts I had, were probably dictated by my abuser and might have made me feel crazy. When someone else's beliefs don't make sense and aren't realistic, and yet that person is constantly telling me they do, I begin to question my way of thinking. I may have believed that I was stupid, ignorant, crazy, or uninformed. When my abuser planted his own thoughts into my head, I began to think his way over time. Today is different because now I can choose my own way of thinking. The best way to begin is to listen to others who have experience in the field of abuse or domestic violence. I will be open to learning all I can about what I've been through, and I will establish my own thoughts and beliefs. I can have my own opinions, my own feelings, and my own values without someone else telling me what they are.

In my healing process, and while changing from behaviors that weren't healthy for me, I might overcompensate. In an effort to recover from codependency, I might appear or feel selfish. When recovering from feeling anxious all the time, I might become too passive. To change a habit of being too lenient, I might find myself being too demanding or inflexible. This change of behavior is like the swinging of a pendulum. Like one in a giant grandfather clock, the pendulum swings from side to side. My behaviors, or the changing of my behaviors, can feel like a pendulum, going from one extreme to the other. Today I will be aware of when I overcompensate with my emotions, reactions, or behaviors. Sometimes it's necessary to experience dramatic change in order to get used to a new and different behavior. I will realize that I don't have to stop there. I can find a balance between the two, knowing when to be lenient and when to say no, when to be concerned and when to be passive. I will allow my emotional pendulum to swing back and forth, finding the balance that is best for me.

Today I will pay attention to the quiet. I will remember the quiet times of my past and what they meant. Did it mean that something was about to happen? Did it mean that my abuser was in one of his good moods, or did it mean I could enjoy the fact that he wasn't home? When did I experience quiet? Was I even aware when it was quiet, or was my focus directed elsewhere? When are the quiet moments in my life now? Do I get time to enjoy quiet reading or some other way of relaxing for myself? How do I feel when it's quiet? Do I turn on the TV or radio for background noise? Do I feel uncomfortable without any sound? Today I will compare the quiet times of my past and my present. I will make an effort to be quiet, have a quiet time, or schedule some time to enjoy the quiet. I can set my alarm for an earlier time, so I can enjoy even ten minutes before others awaken. The quiet times are also good times to pray, meditate, write, or evaluate my day. I can learn to enjoy these times without having to fill them with noise or sound, and I can enjoy them without fear of what they might have meant in the past.

➤ *Day 343*

Resentments are feelings of anger about being treated unjustly, abusively, or wrongfully. Today I will deal with my resentments in an effective, healthy way. I will make a list of resentments that I've thought about more than three times. These most likely involve situations or people with whom I need some kind of closure. I can write letters, whether I mail them or not, and read them to my therapist, my sponsor, a trusted friend, or my support group. I can confront the situation directly, telling the person how I feel about what happened. I can write about my resentments. The most important thing to realize is that if I choose to confront someone, it doesn't always mean that things will be resolved. It may mean that I'll be able to let go of the resentment, and that's it. When I ignore or bury resentments, they will continue to haunt me and prevent me from moving forward. I have to get rid of unwanted anger in order to make room for joy in my life. Unresolved or neglected resentments only keep me in a mind-set of negativity. I look forward to experiencing all the joy I deserve, and I am willing to let go of old resentments in order to have it.

➤ *Day 344*

Today I will determine what it takes to make me feel secure. What is important to my security? Is it having more money? Is it living in a safer neighborhood? Is it having a more stable job? Is it learning new job skills? Is it being able to trust other people? Is it having a phone or pager? Is it having a retirement fund? What are the things that I need in order to feel more secure? I will make a list of these things and focus on them as goals. The most important thing in my life needs to be my safety and the safety of my children. Beyond being safe is feeling secure. I will aim toward creating the most secure environment for my family as possible. It might take some time and certainly some effort on my part, but I'm willing to do the necessary footwork to achieve it. I'm capable of establishing security in my life, and for today, I will better understand what that looks and feels like.

Today I will imagine that I just received $86,400, and I have to spend it all in the next twenty-four hours. How will I use the money? I might choose to pay off my debts or make a large purchase. I might spend it on a vacation or donate some of it to charity. When I decide how I would spend my money, I will evaluate my imaginary spending plan. Did I plan to spend it carefully, or did I spend it all at once? Did I choose to spend it on things that are important to me, which will provide security, or did I opt to spend it on something fun or frivolous? Regardless of what I chose to do, I was able to come up with some kind of plan for spending it. Each day I'm given 86,400 seconds to spend however I choose. How have I been spending those seconds? It is time I will never see again, that I can't save to spend at a later date. It's time that belongs to me, and today I will not waste any of it. In the past, I might have spent too much time worrying about others, trying to please them, being afraid, or walking on eggshells. Today I will use my time in ways that are useful and pleasant to me.

➤ *Day 346*

Uncertainty can be frightening and depressing. When I look ahead with uncertainty, I don't yet know the outcome of a situation, and I'm afraid of what it might be. Even the best plans contain some degree of uncertainty, and life offers no guarantees. Today I will let go of my fears about what might happen and focus on what I can do right now. As long as I've done my best to ensure the safety of myself and my children, I can feel confident in today. No one knows what will happen tomorrow. It is wise to plan ahead and be prepared for it, but I can let go of worrying about what might happen. When I'm comfortable with uncertainty, it means that I'm open to all things, all solutions, all outcomes. It means I'm willing to trust. This might have been difficult in the past, when I lived with an abuser. I might have lived every moment in uncertainty. Today I will look at things differently. Uncertainty is part of life, and I will accept it as part of my life, along with everything else that makes me normal and human.

➤ *Day 347*

Today I will recognize my value. Perhaps in the past I've questioned my value, wondering if I was important, was special, or had something to offer. I might have found value in believing that if I was good enough or tried hard enough, things would change with my abuser. I might have felt valued during the times my abuser was nice to me. My family or children might have valued me, and I felt that my contribution was in keeping us together. Today I will look at the things that made me feel valued in the past and think about what makes me feel valued today. I might instantly know what this is, or I might have to search for the things that make me feel special. Am I a good friend or a caring person? Am I a good and loving mother? Have I done what I could to keep myself and my children safe? Have I reached out to ask for help? Have I opened myself to knowledge or awareness? Have I accomplished something of significance? Any way I've shown courage or willingness to live a life without abuse is valuable. There are many ways I can feel that I'm of value, and today I will focus on what they are.

Grieving is a normal, natural part of life. Every time there is change, there is loss. Even though I may feel happy about my freedom from abuse, there is a sadness I might not understand. I have experienced a loss, and it's normal to feel sad. While I may not feel sad that I've left an abuser, I can be sad about losing a dream I once had. My dream of a loving and nurturing relationship has died. It's okay for me to feel sad about the loss of my dream. It's okay to be angry, sad, confused, or numb. It's normal to feel more than one feeling at the same time, even though they might be opposites. I can be both happy for breaking free of abuse and sad that my dream didn't come true. Something for which I deeply hoped for has died, and it's normal and natural to grieve for it. There is nothing wrong with me if I wish my relationship would have worked out. If I don't understand why I miss my abuser, or why I feel sad, I will remind myself that I might not be sad about leaving him. I might be sad about living with the loss.

➤ *Day 349*

When I listen to others, do I really hear them? Sometimes what someone else is saying sparks an idea or memory, and we stop listening to the speaker because we're planning what we're going to say next. We lose our ability or willingness to really hear others because, in our own minds, we're off in another direction. Today I will practice hearing others. I will listen to what they're saying and really hear them. I will refrain from taking their words and applying them to my own life. I will not try to figure out how I can relate, what's happened in my life that's similar, or how I can respond with my own story. It's impossible for me to fully understand exactly how others feel or think. Even if our situations or experiences are similar, I will never be able to understand exactly how they feel. I will practice hearing others and appreciating that their feelings and thoughts belong to them, and them alone. I can appreciate that when other people talk to me, it's because they want to be heard. It's not necessarily an invitation for me to share something about myself. Today I will begin listening to what other people say, respecting their boundaries and their rights to have their opinions. Just as I want to be heard, I will do the same for others.

➤ Day 350

Have I experienced sadness or intense emotions over some kind of anniversary? Is there a specific day that reminds me of a marriage, a special occasion, a separation, or some other event that no longer holds the same meaning as it did in the past? There may be days that make me feel sentimental or miss my abuser. I don't have to act on these feelings or detour from my healing. I can recognize that I'm grieving a loss, acknowledge that things are different now, and let go of the hope for reconciliation. I can move on in my life, knowing that there are things from my past that I will always remember. Memories don't have to mean going back, fixing the situation, or acting out of regret. I can simply have my memories and the feelings that are attached to them. I might need to write about how it feels to experience the grief or feel the loss. I might even write about what I would like to say to my abuser if I could, but I don't have to say it out loud to him. I can use the resources and tools that I've been given to get through difficult times without returning to old behaviors.

Today I will think of a statement that gives me peace of mind. It might be an affirmation such as "I am lovable," "I am open to good things in my life," "I am receiving everything I need," or "Thy will be done." I may choose to say a mantra from a religion that gives me peace and serenity. Depending on my spiritual beliefs, I can adjust or adapt any statement for this purpose. The idea of saying a positive spiritual statement, affirmation, or mantra is not to receive something by doing so, but to let go, and today I'm willing to let go of anything that isn't for my highest good. A study once was done involving three groups of plants. Daily prayers were said for the first group, asking that they grow strong and tall. The second group was given fertilizer and all the water they needed. For the third group, a simple prayer was said each day: "Thy will be done." After a matter of weeks, the first group was growing nicely. The second group had grown at an average rate. The third group had grown at an outstanding rate and had flourished beyond anyone's expectations. Today I will be open to what is. Thy will be done, and so it is.

➤ *Day 352*

If I were to ask ten people what *beauty* meant to them, I would probably get ten different answers. Beauty means something different to everyone. For some, it can mean physical attractiveness, good looks, sex appeal, innocence, or being pleasing in some way. For others, beauty refers to inner qualities such as being loving and caring, having a sense of values or morals, or being compassionate or honest. It can refer to things we can see, such as the ocean, mountains, an animal, a field of flowers, or the cozy appearance of my home on a cold day. It can refer to qualities we feel: comfort, satisfaction, appreciation, anticipation, or peace. Today I will recognize what I view as beauty. I will notice the things around me that I find beautiful and the qualities inside me that give me beauty. I will pay closer attention to that which is attractive and desirable, using all of my senses.

Today I will choose how I want to appear to others. If I wish, I can create an appearance that shows how I feel about my sexuality. Have I ever been told how to dress or prevented from expressing myself in my appearance? Did I have to buy certain types of clothing because someone else told me to? Did I wish I could look different, but couldn't because of someone else's insecurities or beliefs? Today I will look the way that best expresses my inner self. Have I wanted to look more feminine? Have I wished I could look more masculine? Have I limited my appearance to one type of look or fashion? Today I will do one thing that changes the way I express my sexuality. I can paint my fingernails, wear makeup, or wear a skirt that makes me feel more feminine. I can buy an outfit that is more stylish or one that makes me feel more attractive. I can fix my hair in ways that express my inner self. I can change the way I appear to others and decide what my appearance says about me. Today I will be more comfortable about my sexuality and not be afraid to show it. As I become more comfortable with who I am on the inside, it will become easier to make changes on the outside.

➤ Day 354

Inspiration is usually defined as a sudden act of creativity or an idea. Today I will be open to inspiration, and I will open my mind to creative ideas. I can choose to write poetry or a short story, paint or draw a picture, take up a hobby, try a new recipe, write a song, redecorate my bedroom, make a quilt from old clothes, take photographs, plant a garden, or any other creative endeavor in which I can experience being inspired. Being creative will help me focus on something besides my problems or challenges, and it will open my mind to new ways of thinking. In the past, my creative outlet may have been making excuses or rationalizing my situation. Today I will take that energy and use it for something more positive. If I don't have a creative outlet yet, I will try different things until I find something that is fun for me. I will allow myself to be inspired. Even if I don't believe I'll be successful, I will still make a promise to try it.

➤ Day 355

The tides of the ocean go out and then come back in. There's nothing I can do to change it. The tides are the way they are because of circumstances beyond my control. Sometimes things happen that can't be changed or stopped. Today I will accept this as part of life, as part of the human experience. Even though I will do my best to handle the challenges I must face, I will accept the fact that there will be circumstances I can do nothing about. When they happen, I will experience all my emotions. I can experience joy to the same degree that I experience fear. I can appreciate that I feel sad to the same degree that I appreciate my happiness. Anger serves a purpose that is just as important as cheerfulness. I don't have to stifle certain emotions because they make me feel uncomfortable, yet I don't have to wallow in them either. I can accept each emotion as part of my life, realize I can't stop it, and then move on to the next one. Today I will be glad for my emotions and feelings. I can be glad for feeling them because it means I'm alive and well.

➤ Day 356

Today I will understand the difference between being assertive and being aggressive. When I act in an aggressive manner, I may appear to be abrasive, closed-minded, controlling, bossy, and unwilling to listen to others. Aggressive people are usually offensive and appear to know only one way to get what they want. They tell others what to do, what they want, and how they want it. Assertive people, on the other hand, stand up for themselves, set boundaries, express their feelings, ask for what they want, and try to come to an understanding with others. Some people consider assertive people to be aggressive, believing they should remain "in their place" or in traditional roles or stereotypes. It is okay for me to ask for what I want, state my boundaries, and express my feelings. In the past, I was probably not permitted to do so, or if I did, I was told to stop or was abused for it. Today I will understand that I have the right to be assertive, and I will continue to practice my assertiveness without being aggressive.

When I feel confused about my feelings and wonder how I can feel two opposing feelings at the same time, I will understand that it's a normal experience. I can be happy about a new job and be afraid at the same time. I can feel sad over a loss but glad about the change at the same time. I can feel excited about being independent and feel worried about it at the same time. It's normal to experience two feelings simultaneously that aren't similar at all. I don't need to be concerned over which one is right or which one is wrong. They're both right. Today I will realize that my feelings are always right no matter what they are, because even though thoughts or perceptions might not be accurate, my feelings always are.

➤ Day 358

When my life has changed for the better and everything around me is moving in a positive direction, I might not know how to accept it. I might be used to feeling unhappy, being mistreated, being the victim, or feeling miserable. Then, one day, I realize how good everything is, and I'm surprised that I'm not feeling happier. It's probably because I'm not accustomed to a lifestyle that feels this good. These are new feelings for me, and I have to remind myself that this is what I've been waiting for, planning for, and working for. I am finally seeing it happen. I might be caught off-guard by this realization, but today I will enjoy it as a precious gift. Today I will be open to seeing the goodness in my life as a reward for my hard work. Even if I don't recognize it right away, I'll recognize that I'm now able to see it and feel it instead of just hoping for it.

Now that I've learned how to recognize abusive people by using intuition, red flags, and past experiences, I will realize that some people aren't necessarily abusive, but can be difficult to be around. Some people are moody, negative, nosy, bossy, aggressive, irresponsible, dishonest, or manipulative, and yet, they are not abusive. If I know people who are difficult to be with, I will try to accept them for who they are, but I'll continue to set my boundaries and stand up for myself. Sometimes I can tolerate difficult people better if I recognize their negative tendencies but don't allow them to have power over me. Even if I find an employer or manager offensive, I can find a way to accept that person's character defects as long as no abuse is occurring. It doesn't mean I have to be friends with difficult people or see them socially. It means that I can recognize qualities in others that I don't agree with, refrain from trying to change them, set an example, and let it go. Today I will accept people for who they are, whether they're pleasant or annoying, and remember that the only person I can change is me.

With my newly found knowledge and awareness, I may become upset, frustrated, or angry when people I care about are making obvious mistakes. I might tell them what I think, offer my opinion, or speak from experience. It doesn't mean they're going to listen, however. When other people have not yet learned from their mistakes, it can be hard for me to watch. I can accept that other people might not make decisions that are good for them, and I can love them anyway. Just because I've learned how to make wiser decisions, others don't have to listen to me and follow my advice. I can know in my heart that what I have to say is valuable. I can know that they'd probably be better off if they listened. Knowing that my opinions and advice would be helpful doesn't mean I'll be able to help. Today I will remember a time when I wasn't ready to hear good advice and acknowledge how painful that must have felt for people who love me. I can continue to love those who are close to me and allow them the room to learn from their mistakes. I can tell them that I'm concerned for them and that I wish they'd do things differently, but I can continue to love them in their process.

➤ *Day 361*

Today I will remember not to criticize other people
when they don't make the same decisions I would
make. Even though my way of thinking has
changed for the better, other people may still not
be capable of making wise or informed decisions. I
won't criticize people who are not like me. We all
learn at our own pace, and we heal in our own
ways. Some people want to experience healing, and
others do not. Some people seek counseling,
support groups, therapy, or some sort of mentor,
and others do not. Some people want to talk about
their problems, work them out, and resolve them.
Others might simply choose to try to forget their
problems and put them in the past. They probably
don't realize that by doing this, they will experience
little healing or growth, and their problems will
continue to arise. Even though I know this, I will
not criticize others for making the choices they
make. The only decisions I should be concerned
about are mine.

➤ Day 362

I've made mistakes and will continue to make mistakes. Everybody makes mistakes. The difference now is that I can see them more clearly afterward, and I am not living in denial about them. If I become too critical of myself when I do make a mistake, I can remind myself that it's part of being human. I can remind myself that it's a learning experience and a mistake I won't make so easily in the future. Mistakes are not made intentionally, but they are errors caused by a lack of information or lack of attention. Today I pay attention more than ever before and have more information than I ever have had. Mistakes will still happen, but they probably won't be as serious or dangerous as they were in my past. I can allow myself to make mistakes, understanding that when I give myself this freedom, I am accepting myself for who I am and loving myself unconditionally.

➤ Day 363

Today I will be open to the beauty of my life. I will enjoy simple pleasures: the morning sun, the food I eat, the clothes I wear, the warmth of the day, a breeze, water when I'm thirsty, my body, my willingness, my open mind. I will enjoy everything around me that makes my life what it is. I will enjoy the absence of fear. I will enjoy knowing that no one is going to hit me, threaten me, or hurt me today. I will look at what I have achieved and what I've gained, and I will fall in love with my capacity for kindness and my loving spirit. I will be open to feeling the magnificence of faith, the willingness to trust, and the care of my guiding lights, whomever they have been. Today I will feel loved, for I deserve it, just as I've always deserved it. Today I will be empowered by the knowledge that real love—true love—doesn't have to hurt.

➤ *Day 364*

My healing requires a combination of thoughts, emotions, feelings, reactions, learning, and personal growth. I've experienced all of these and have learned from each one. Today I will use my knowledge to determine where to draw the line in current and future experiences. If someone makes a comment that triggers a feeling or response reminding me of my past, I will decide to deal with it appropriately. Have I healed enough simply to let it go, or are there unresolved issues I still need to address? Do I need to tell this person how I feel? Am I able to recognize and understand uncomfortable feelings that are caused by the pain of my past? Am I able to accept my emotions, acknowledge them, and come back into the present moment? Can I realize that what's happening now is very different from what happened in the past? When I'm able to do all of this, I might even find some comments to be funny or humorous. When I develop the skills to stay out of the past, I will be a more receptive and better listener now. Even if the words are the same, the tone and intent can be different. Today I will accept that my healing process has brought me to a place of new and different reactions.

➤ *Day 365*

Today is my New Year's Eve. In the time it took to read this book, approximately 3,503,000 women were battered. Thanks to my willingness and determination, and to everyone who was there for me, I was not one of them. Today I will fly free into a new year for myself. I will dress up, make reservations at a restaurant, cook a nice meal, buy confetti, make streamers, get party hats and horns, or make a quiet toast to myself. It is my New Year's Eve because one year ago today, I opened this book and began my journey toward living without abuse, making the commitment never to live that way again. It's a new year, a new beginning, a new way of living, and in it there exists a new me. Today I will celebrate the newness of my life. Happy new year to the most wondrous, magnificent, extraordinary person I've come to know: me.

Today I will feel my wings. While I was being abused, my wings had been clipped, which prevented me from moving forward in my life and discovering who I am. In these past twelve months, I've become more aware of what I'm capable of achieving. I learned valuable lessons, including how to soar above the problems of my past. I've met new people and friends, and I've faced difficult challenges that I'm now able to overcome. Today I will understand what it means to fly free. I will experience the new me—the person I've become—and fly above the pain I once felt. There were probably many times when I couldn't feel my wings, and it was during these times that I was taken under the wings of others. They may have been people in my support group, my therapist, my sponsor, a close friend, a women's advocate, or someone I had chosen as my teacher. Most important, I was always under the wing of my Spiritual Power. Through all the hurt and confusion, feelings of unworthiness, and doubts about myself, one thing remained true: My teachers all held me close until my own wings became strong enough to take me to a place of discovery, where I learned that I was a child worth loving.

➤ Suggested Reading

Beattie, Melody. *Beyond Codependency: And Getting Better All the Time.* Center City, Minn.: Hazelden, 1989.

———. *Codependent No More: How to Stop Controlling Others and Start Caring for Yourself.* 2d ed. Center City, Minn.: Hazelden, 1992.

———. *The Language of Letting Go.* Center City, Minn.: Hazelden, 1990.

Engel, Beverly. *Encouragements for the Emotionally Abused Woman: Wisdom and Hope for Women at Any Stage of Emotional Abuse Recovery.* New York: Fawcett Columbine, 1993.

NiCarthy, Ginny. *Getting Free: You Can End Abuse and Take Back Your Life.* Seattle: Seal Press, 1997.

NiCarthy, Ginny, and Sue Davidson. *You Can Be Free: An Easy-to-Read Handbook for Abused Women.* Seattle: Seal Press, 1997.

Renzetti, Claire. *Violent Betrayal: Partner Abuse in Lesbian Relationships.* Newbury Park, Calif.: Sage Publications, 1992.

Smith, Judith R. *Time to Break Free: Meditations for the First 100 Days after Leaving an Abusive Relationship.* Center City, Minn.: Hazelden, 1999.

Statman, Jan Berliner. *The Battered Woman's Survival Guide: Breaking the Cycle.* Dallas: Taylor Publishing, 1995.

Weldon, Michele. *I Closed My Eyes: Revelations of a Battered Woman.* Center City, Minn.: Hazelden, 1999.

White, Evelyn C. *Chain Chain Change: For Black Women in Abusive Relationships.* Seattle: Seal Press, 1994.

Zambrano, Myra M. *Mejor Sola Que Mal Acompañada: Para la Mujer Golpeada* (for the Latina in an abusive relationship). Seattle: Seal Press, 1985.

➤ Resources

Battered Women's Justice Project
Criminal Justice Center
4032 Chicago Avenue South
Minneapolis, MN 55407
(800) 903-0111

National Council on Child Abuse and Family Violence
1155 Connecticut Avenue Northwest, Suite 400
Washington, DC 20036
(800) 799-7233
(202) 429-6695

National Domestic Abuse Hotline
(800) 799-SAFE (7223)
TDD (800) 787-3224

National Victim Center
2111 Wilson Boulevard, Suite 300
Arlington, VA 22201
(800) FYI-CALL (394-2255)
Provides information and referrals, not crisis counseling.

WOMAN, Inc.
333 Valencia Street, Suite 251
San Francisco, CA 94103
(415) 864-4722
For lesbians in violent relationships.

➤ Index

Each number reflects the day of the meditation.

Judith R. Smith experienced one abusive relationship after another beginning at the age of sixteen. Her relationships included emotional and verbal abuse, and many times they became physically abusive. At the age of thirty-eight, she realized that she had once again become involved with another abuser. In December 1994, her abuser threw a recliner across the room, sent the children to their rooms, and threatened to kill Judith. It was then that she realized nothing was ever going to change, her hopes of a better life with this man would never come true, and she had to save her children from the nightmare they were living. She knew she had to leave.

As her abuser's rage continued, Judith quietly planned her escape. When he finally left the house, she gathered her two young children and a few clothes, and she drove away. She knew she would not be back. Over the next few weeks, she continued to talk to her abuser on the phone, listening to his promises that things would be better and that he would try harder, and when that didn't work, his threats. She began attending a support group for battered women twice a week, and did so for nine months. She discovered that she was not alone, that there were other people who cared and who were willing to help her, and that what she had experienced for so long had a name. She was suffering from battered woman syndrome, which often occurs in domestic violence situations. She listened to others who had once been in abusive relationships, and she noticed the similarities. She realized that her abuser wasn't different from other abusers, and the dynamics of domestic violence were the same in all abusive relationships. Judith realized that if she were to break the pattern of abuse, she would have to realize what attracted her to abusive men and make a change. She knew she would have to relearn the meaning of real love, because her perception of it had been wrong for as long as she could remember.

Judith began attending classes and became a battered women's advocate. Her certificate qualified her to work in a shelter or on a domestic violence hot line, but she decided to use her personal experience, knowledge, and training to write books for people, like herself, who wanted to live a life without abuse. After completing *Time to Break Free: Meditations for the First 100 Days after Leaving an Abusive Relationship*, Judith wanted to write a book for people who were looking for more. She realized that abusive people aren't always domestic partners or spouses. Abuse lies within the workplace, within friendships, and within just about any kind of relationship. In this book, Judith has written supportive, enlightening, and helpful suggestions as well as information about healing from abuse, setting boundaries, recognizing when a relationship might be abusive, dealing with abusive employers, parenting, and choosing and maintaining healthy relationships.

At the time of this book's publishing, Judith has been free of any type of abuse for six years. She is proud to be an ex-battered woman, having found the courage, strength, support, and commitment to live a life without abuse, no matter what. She has extensive experience as a teacher, artist, public speaker, writer, and mother, her most cherished accomplishment. Judith currently resides in California, where she enjoys a loving and healthy relationship with a man who appreciates her for who she truly is. She has learned that after the healing comes the reward of knowing what real love is. She provides a loving and nurturing home for her two children, where they are encouraged to express themselves freely and without fear. She has taught them to accept nothing less than to be treated with respect and kindness, and she has given them the skills to deal with their anger in appropriate ways. By her example, Judith continues to show her children that any kind of abuse is wrong and that we all deserve to live lives in which we feel safe and loved.

Hazelden Information and Educational Services is a division of the Hazelden Foundation, a not-for-profit organization. Since 1949, Hazelden has been a leader in promoting the dignity and treatment of people afflicted with the disease of chemical dependency.

The mission of the foundation is to improve the quality of life for individuals, families, and communities by providing a national continuum of information, education, and recovery services that are widely accessible; to advance the field through research and training; and to improve our quality and effectiveness through continuous improvement and innovation.

Stemming from that, the mission of this division is to provide quality information and support to people wherever they may be in their personal journey—from education and early intervention, through treatment and recovery, to personal and spiritual growth.

Although our treatment programs do not necessarily use everything Hazelden publishes, our bibliotherapeutic materials support our mission and the Twelve Step philosophy upon which it is based. We encourage your comments and feedback.

The headquarters of the Hazelden Foundation are in Center City, Minnesota. Additional treatment facilities are located in Chicago, Illinois; New York, New York; Plymouth, Minnesota; St. Paul, Minnesota; and West Palm Beach, Florida. At these sites, we provide a continuum of care for men and women of all ages. Our Plymouth facility is designed specifically for youth and families.

For more information on Hazelden, please call 1-800-257-7800. Or you may access our World Wide Web site on the Internet at www.hazelden.org.